simply irresistible

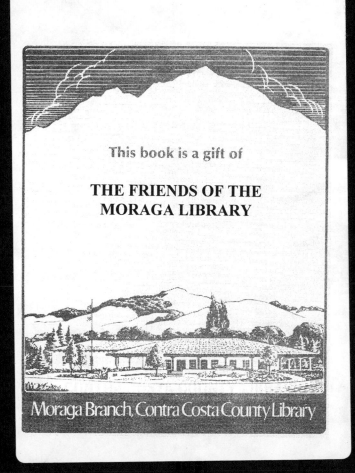

To Mathilde and Mollie Brent
with thanks to Paul Dixon

9   8   7   6   5   4   3   2   1
Digit on the right indicates the number of this printing

Library of Congress Control Number: 2007920532

ISBN-13: 978-0-7624-2673-7
ISBN-10: 0-7624-2673-X

Interior design by Susan Van Horn
Edited by Diana C. von Glahn
Typography: Horley Old Style, Lauren Script and Cronos

This book may be ordered by mail from the publisher.
Please include $2.50 for postage and handling.
But try your bookstore first!

Running Press Book Publishers
2300 Chestnut Street
Philadelphia, PA 19103-4371

Visit us on the web!
www.runningpress.com

table of contents

"I don't want to live—I want to love first, and live incidentally."

—*Zelda Fitzgerald*

preface

It has long been my ambition to write a how-to book on romance. Not for me the Great American Novel or a definitive history—my fascination is for the details of people's romantic lives. I never fail to ask a couple how they first met, and what attracted them to each other the most. For me, the sentence "I met an interesting man" is the beginning of hours of delightful speculation.

I come from a long line of women who treated seduction dead seriously—and who remained successful in their pursuits as long as they had a breath in their bodies. In my immediate family alone, my grandmother, at fifty-six, wooed a younger man out of bachelorhood after she had been twice widowed. My mother, whose yearbook picture bore the legend "wolverine," still entertained gentleman callers when she was seventy-five. But within the context of my family, I was a particularly slow starter. When I was a mere ten or eleven years old, my grandmother became so concerned that boys were not showing the expected level of interest in me that she and my mother sat me down for a talk. Up until that time, I was an obedient little girl with a straight A average—a credit to any other family. But dates with boys? They actually expected me to have dates? I didn't even have breasts.

So it was under two generations of maternal guidance that I tossed aside my schoolwork and boned up on my flirtation techniques. It was rough going. As I sat cross-legged and alert in my stiff school uniform, my grandmother advised me in the delivery of "come hither" remarks that make me writhe with embarrassment even today. Her personal favorite was, "I dreamt about you last night," which she said should be communicated with an air of mystery. "What if he asks what I dreamt?" I asked earnestly—a question that invited her obvious disdain at my lack of imagination. When, at eighteen, I finally worked up the nerve to use that line at a garden party, a bird flying overhead took strategic relief on my forearm.

Still, while my progress was slow, I had a respectable collection of semi-besotted teenaged suitors by the time I was sixteen. My first boyfriend, Pete, wrote me poetry every day while I was away at school and signed all his letters "Te quiero" ("I love you" in Spanish). I had a smattering of summer romances with boys from Long Island, Boston, and Iowa, with whom I subsequently corresponded. But the year I inspired a barroom-style brawl between two guys who ended up spending the night in jail, I began to feel I had stumbled into the *zone*. News of my "triumph" was broadcast within my family, who acted as if I had just won a Rhodes scholarship—and in their view, I suppose I had.

Armed with my beginner's success and a keen eye for the great romantic story, I studied the masters. I had read a few of F. Scott Fitzgerald's novels and learned that his heroines were modeled on Zelda Sayre, the legendary Southern belle who became his wife. I bought several of her biographies. Later, I developed an interest in Jennie Jerome—the American society girl who later became the mother of Winston Churchill. Not only did Jennie keep Victorian England agog with her romantic exploits, but she closed out her active career with a marriage to a contemporary of her son's. Then came my interest in Cleopatra, the courtesan Veronica Franco, and Pamela Harriman, among many, many others.

All of this made for instructive and fascinating reading, but it was hard to

So many men, so little time.

grasp the essence of what made these women irresistible to men without seeing them in action. I understood that Jennie's wit was part of her great appeal, but if wit was all a girl needed, then wouldn't Whoopi Goldberg be constantly fending off marriage proposals? And though I'd read that Pamela Harriman seduced some of the world's most powerful men by hanging on their every word, didn't that make her somewhat of a doormat?

Years later, when I was living in Washington, D.C., I met a contemporary femme fatale named Ruth Vogel. By almost any standard of measurement, Ruth was plain—flat-chested and skinny, with stringy blonde hair, a big nose, and beady little eyes. Yet her whole being projected the conviction that she was a raving beauty. Guys never seemed to be able to catch up with her, or at least she made them feel that way. She had a kind of goddess quality, I observed—alluring yet distant and untouchable, though she was always in the close company of men. In addition, she had individual traits that heightened her appeal. She was unusually smart—an intellectual, really, who wowed men with her mental agility. And she was always beautifully dressed in clothes that were contemporary, yet somehow suggested another, more romantic decade. She was elusive, either way ahead of them, or back somewhere in another time, and men were driven to rash and near-suicidal acts over her. I watched in awe.

Through Ruth's example, I began to understand some fundamental truths. While it helps to be beautiful, it's not *essential* to being irresistible to men, and beauty alone is not enough. Men are most attracted to women who are convinced of their own appeal—the *sine qua non* of the irresistible woman. And, while it may go without saying, these women love men. Furthermore, they live large, as if men and life were created for their pleasure. After further consideration, I saw that Sirens fall roughly into five distinguishable archetypes—namely, the Goddess, the Companion, the Sex Kitten, the Competitor, and the Mother—based on their dominant qualities. Building on this foundation, the irresistible woman will have her series of individual quirks, tricks, and talents that personalize and heighten her appeal, creating her own signature "brand."

Over the years I've inspired my modest share of marriage proposals, infatuations, bad poetry, and even a novel in which I figured—albeit unflatteringly—as a love interest, but I consider myself to be more of a passionate student of the genre. And *Simply Irresistible* is my thesis on the subject. This book will give you a blueprint for becoming a Siren, using notably seductive women as case histories, providing invaluable and timeless lessons in love. More than being simply irresistible, the Sirens who populate these pages are women of substance—interesting and admirable people outside the context of their romantic exploits. As women who have gotten much of what they want out of life, they are well worth studying.

PART ONE

finding your inner siren

SIREN QUEST

So you want to be a Siren. Or if not a Siren exactly, you want to channel some of her power over men into your life. Maybe you have one man in mind, or more intriguingly, a bevy. Well, you've come to the right place. Within these pages, the collective wisdom of some of the great Sirens of history has been distilled to its essence and embellished with homespun lore from the awesome, lesser-known seductresses of my acquaintance. Maybe you'll borrow a page, a chapter, or a few of these lessons in love. Maybe you'll become a disciple.

But aren't Sirens born, you ask, not made? 'Taint necessarily so. The Siren's power lies within each of us. She is part of our most primal selves, if we can only seize the courage to unleash her. Deep down, we all have the power to attract—to strut, crow, spread our feathers, and bring men shuddering to their knees. But first, we need to identify and personalize the qualities that make us so alluring. *Simply Irresistible* peels back the layers and exposes it all.

We begin by learning who the Siren is, along with her core values—the launching pad for lessons in love. We'll move on to study the archetypes—Goddess, Companion, Sex Kitten, Competitor, and Mother—using some of the greats as role models. Finally, we'll layer on attributes that individualize your appeal. You'll learn how Sirens create a signature style, why they are unforgettable, how they transport men—sexually or otherwise—and how you can do and be the same.

Our study is not frivolous. The advantages of being a Siren are not just about men, love, and sex appeal, as if they were not enough. In 1000 BC or in AD 2010, the rules for ordinary mortals do not apply to Sirens. This is in part because the Siren refuses to see the accepted mores of what nice girls do and don't do. And to the Siren, refusing to see obstacles often means that they just aren't there. But more to the point: in a man's world, the Siren's power is such that she almost always gets her own way—through her own brand of irresistible style and charm. The Siren calls the shots, and no one dares to stop her. And you do want to call the shots, don't you?

A PRIMER: THE BIRTH OF THE SIREN

The Siren's story begins in ancient Greece, with the beleaguered action hero Odysseus, who trudged dutifully through twelve chapters of Homer's epic poem *The Odyssey*. My memory of studying *The Odyssey* is indistinct, as I routinely got through school assignments on a phalanx of hastily read CliffsNotes®. It's safe to say that Odysseus' journey around the world was long, tediously grueling, and fraught with dangers that you and I can only dream about—quite literally. Not the least of these perils was his encounter with the mythical Sirens, recognizable as half bird, half woman, and all bad news.

Odysseus' sorceress pal Circe had warned him about the lethal enchantment of the Sirens' song. Perched on an island in the western sea between Aeaea and the rocks of Scylla (i.e., somewhere off the coast of Italy), the Sirens warbled to passing sailors. So seductive was their call that men would forget their homes, wives, and children, and make a beeline for these bird-like babes. Inevitably, the men would meet their untimely deaths on the rocks. But Odysseus took Circe's advice and, while his men plugged up their ears with wax, he ordered them to tie their gallant captain—ears unplugged—to the mast, so he could hear the Sirens' song. They passed unscathed, and the rest, as they say, is history, or rather, classical myth.

THE SIREN TODAY

Today's Siren is a woman who, by some mysterious combination of qualities, is irresistible to men. Not all men, necessarily. Not each man, every time. But a Siren's batting average is very high. We know these women as the man-eaters of history, from Cleopatra to Angelina Jolie. And, unrecognized by posterity, they live among us. Even without meaning to, Sirens play men off each other, break their hearts, bring them to unaccustomed tears, and cause them to commit rash acts. A Siren owns the room—or at least most of the men in it—when she walks in. Without singing a note, she has a song, and men will scramble over whatever lies in their way to listen.

Being a Siren is not being a babe, or a bombshell, or a hottie—though being any of the aforementioned does not exempt you from becoming a Siren. And you don't necessarily have to be young, buff, or smartly turned out. In fact, let me go out on a limb here: being physically exceptional can sometimes be a deterrent to becoming a world-class Siren—Helen of Troy notwithstanding. Being beautiful is too easy. Everyone naturally gravitates toward beautiful people; consequently, beautiful people are rarely forced to spend any time or thought on becoming magnetic people or in calculating how to get what they want. And Sirens are nothing if not calculating. Sirens rely on the force of their personalities to make the world take notice.

The essence of a Siren's song is, and always will be, sex appeal—a quality for which beauty is only a decorative effect. "Sex appeal doesn't depend entirely on physical attributes," said the actress Dorothy Dandridge, quite rightly. "It's a kind of vitality and energy . . . it has to do with how you feel as a person." Diana Vreeland might have been talking about a Siren when she said, "you don't have to be beautiful to be wildly attractive." The roster of Sirens is filled with women who were not only without physical charms, but were downright plain—the Duchess of Windsor, the courtesan Cora Pearl, and the singer Edith Piaf, just to mention a few.

HAVE ABSOLUTE CONFIDENCE IN YOUR ALLURE

The Siren may doubt her abilities in other areas, but she has absolute faith in the irresistible force of her appeal to men. She was born with this unshakeable confidence, and it keeps her smokin', even when it's cold. After all, just like the rest of us, Sirens have bad hair days and overdrawn checking accounts—and they even occasionally get trumped by other Sirens. The Hollywood glamour puss Slim Keith, for example, lost her second husband to the inestimable Pamela Churchill (later Harriman), and Pam forfeited Fiat heir Gianni Agnelli to an Italian heiress. But to a Siren, it's the amorous successes that resonate. She treats her low moments as aberrations and her triumphs as gospel.

Surely, you've witnessed the phenomenon of the woman who, for no evident reason, is so taken with her own beauty, talent, or sense of self-importance that she hoodwinks the world. Even those who are not hoodwinked somehow manage to go along. "She's so beautiful and smart," I remember often hearing about an acquaintance with this kind of impenetrable confidence. I had (perhaps a little cattily) observed that the woman in question had a *derriere* the size of a private heliport and a penchant for restating the abundantly obvious as if it were news just in from Mensa. Didn't anyone else notice? This Washington political hostess, as she was, so intrigued an Arab king (and a major-league one at that) that he showered her with expensive gifts, among them a white Arabian stallion. Is there a woman alive who wouldn't like to flaunt an Arabian stallion as proof of her appeal? For the Siren, there seems to be no end to the power of this kind of positive thinking.

To truly be a Siren, you need to decide that you too are fantastically irresistible, even if it requires the same crazy leap of faith that you might draw on to suddenly become a redhead. You need to make this decision over your own most strenuous and reasoned objections. The evidence is slim, you say? The jury's still out? Well, you're missing the point. As you must know by now, it's the confidence *itself* that's the draw. Don't look for the evidence of your appeal—create it with your towering self-regard. Even if you have to fake it. Treat it like a performance, and dress the part. Persuade yourself that you beat men off with a stick. You'll find that confidence in motion stays in motion and carries everybody in its gravitational field.

CELEBRATE MEN

Sirens never begin sentences with "the problem with men is. . . ." Nor do they trade jokes that suggest that men are the inferior sex (unless they're really, *really* funny). And God forbid that they should have books on their shelves with titles like *Men Who Hate Women and the Women Who Love Them.* (Time for spring cleaning?) The plain truth is that Sirens love men—individually, as a group, practically as a religious persuasion—way too much to think ill of them. Indeed, they strongly identify with men. And basking in that high regard, men have allowed these alluring women to twist them any which way. But while a Siren will often prefer the company of a man, she would never, ever choose to be one. She thinks it's a damn shame that men can't share in all the fun she has being a woman.

Life for the Siren is there to be embraced, in all its variations, along with the men in it. But she especially enjoys the power that comes with getting the undivided attention of men. In fact, she's a tiny bit addicted to that attention—it is part of who she is. Take men away from the Siren, and you'll still have a formidable, fascinating human being, just not a particularly fulfilled one. To Gloria

Steinem's declaration that "a woman needs a man like a fish needs a bicycle," the Siren says "have you got one built for two, or, better still, three?"

So delete those male-bashing e-mails. Put an end to late night complaint sessions. See men in all their flawed glory as your best friends and brothers. Look for reasons to celebrate men and to get all gooey behind your hard candy shell. Though male-bashing may be the shibboleth of the politically correct woman, be the first on your block to buck the trend. If men are from Mars and women are from Venus, in the Siren's world, the planets merge.

SIRENS CELEBRATE MEN

Man and woman are two locked caskets,
of which each contains the key to the other.
—*Isak Dinesen*

One of the best things about love is just recognizing
a man's step when he climbs the stairs.
—*Colette*

Men ought to be more conscious of
their bodies as an object of delight.
—*Germaine Greer*

Men make love more intensely at twenty,
but make love better, however, at thirty.
—*Catherine the Great*

I feel like a million tonight—but one at a time.
—*Mae West*

Of course, old habits *do* die hard, and you may struggle with turning an old attitude into something shiny and new. It might help you to hear something about my Siren grandmother's approach. Even as a little girl, I knew she held women to much higher standards than men, and men always got the benefit of the doubt. My brother had only to show his cherubic face to get first prize, whereas she was always faintly disappointed if I didn't have something clever to say. When I was a teenager, she gave me a little insight. "Women have all that natural emotional intelligence, and men are given only blunt instruments," she said, as if this was self-evident, "but they are such delightful creatures. Try to be a little forgiving." In matters of the heart and human relations—the only world she felt really mattered—my grandmother held that women possessed the superior tools. She advised using them kindly.

EMBRACE LIFE

Be she a kook, character, sexpot, intellectual, muse, mother, or moll, the Siren lives large. Each embraces life in her own way and is determined to live it as thoroughly as possible. "I love life, I love people," said Lady Randolph Churchill (Winston's mother) when, in her mid-sixties, she was asked to explain her popularity with younger men. "I have known all the world has to give—ALL!" confessed the scandalous courtesan Lola Montez on her deathbed.

Though her very existence may hinge on a man (as would have often been the case before the twentieth century), the Siren makes the most of her little corner of the world, managing to embellish it in her own swashbuckling style. I like to cite Margaretha Geertruida Zelle, who reinvented herself as the early twentieth-century siren and spy Mata Hari. Orphaned, shuffled off to relatives, and married young to a violent stranger in the Dutch West Indies, she came back at life as a "sacred dancer from a Ganges temple" within the salons of Paris. As she lived, so she left the world. At her execution on trumped-up charges of treason during World War I, Mata Hari, dressed to the nines, blew a kiss at her firing squad and smiled, causing one soldier to faint and another to marvel, "*Sacre bleu*, this lady knows how to die." A contemporary Siren, the singer Tina Turner, also has a vitality and larger-than-life quality that can't be suppressed.

Risk a little rejection. Let go of the extraneous details. Try remembering that the only thing you have to fear is not fear, actually, but yourself. Embrace your life as if you were the beneficiary of a windfall profit, even as a tax auditor is knocking at your door. Begin as you might any project: draw up the proverbial list of things large and small that make your life embraceable. In no time, you'll find yourself as cheerful as that mad nun Maria in *The Sound of Music* (though you'll want to resist the urge to remake the drapes into clothes that blend with the upholstery).

To get you started, here is a short list (Siren style) of things that make life embraceable, in no particular order:

+ New clothes that give you confidence.
+ Traveling to an exotic location and broadening your world view.
+ Having someone fall so deeply in love with you that he'd willingly make a fool of himself.
+ Realizing that you've gotten really good at doing something, even if it's hospital corners on bed sheets.
+ Good books that both carry you away and teach you something new.
+ The ocean and the mountains—the reality and the idea.
+ Working really, really hard at something and getting results.
+ Friendships that somehow survive.
+ Being unexpectedly moved by anything.
+ Food that transports you, even if it's Jujubes with a popcorn chaser.

the allure of archetypes

How did Eva Perón seduce a nation? Did Greta Garbo really want to be alone, or was she trying to make them sweat? And why, many wonder, did Pamela Harriman prevail over more attractive women? The basis of their appeal, my friends, lies in their archetype.

Sirens are, of course, a proud breed of individuals. But like the sports car with a sturdy chassis, each Siren's character is built on a solid foundation—her working archetype. Sirens come in five varieties, namely, the Goddess, the Companion, the Sex Kitten, the Competitor, and the Mother, and those categories roughly correspond to primal male needs (after food, shelter, and a close shave). If you doubt me, ponder the oft-touted Mother Figure. It is no news that men never fully outgrow the need to be mothered, regardless of how evolved they may be. They are hardwired for it, just as women are set up to expect the arrival of their paternal "white knight."

Beyond mothering, men need to connect, to conquer, and to dream—not to mention, to create and multiply. Without necessarily even knowing how they come by their ability, Sirens satisfy, on some level, those ancient desires.

It goes something like this:

SIREN	PRIMAL MALE DESIRE
Goddess	*To Dream*
Companion	*To Connect (Validation)*
Sex Kitten	*To Create (Multiply)*
Competitor	*To Conquer (or Tame)*
Mother	*To Be Nurtured*

Though each Siren is predominantly a single archetype, she can mix it up, borrowing from other categories—as in, the Goddess Siren may be in part a Competitor. Or, ever versatile, she will bring her mothering skills to bear if the situation demands. And, regardless of archetype, every Siren knows when to draw on her inner Sex Kitten. The Siren's talent for rising to the challenge lies in her highly developed empathy for men and her intuitive ability to apply those skills. But the men who are attracted to, for instance, a Goddess Siren are chiefly drawn by the dominant qualities of her archetype, such as her mystery and/or her other-worldliness. These chapters explore the archetypes, using some of the world's most famous Sirens as case studies. Aspiring Sirens can learn much from the experts and should choose their behavior to achieve their ends.

the goddess

Who isn't familiar with the lure of the unattainable—that man who would complete us if he only knew we were alive? Only those of us who have spent time in the fetal position can know the exquisite pain and pleasure of pining for the one we can't have. But if women have it bad, men have it worse. The Goddess Siren pushes the buttons of his desire by keeping a part of herself tantalizingly out of reach. Try as he might to shake himself loose, he can't get over her. The closest I can ever come to being a Goddess Siren is when I have no interest in a man at all—and I never cease to be amazed by how well it works. The first time I had a taste of this, I was sixteen and vacationing with my parents. I met a boy who was unable to resist my charms, and I, naturally, was smitten with someone else. I treated him like a lowly cabana boy, which only spurred him on. On our last night, I refused to kiss him goodbye. I later learned that he had been captivated by my (ha!) "independence." Of course, if I'd been interested, he would have had to pry me loose.

The Goddess archetype is not so much about sex as it is about the seductive appeal of distance. She stokes man's conviction that the perfect woman exists. And, of course, that dream stays vividly alive as long as she's not wholly his. The Goddess eats, sleeps, and picks her teeth like other mortals, but she manages to project an otherworldly glow. If he is the dreamer, she is the dream. And because she is in love with the myth herself, their fantasy is a synchronized dance.

The Goddess Siren's detachment is part of her nature. Many Sirens, however, work a little Goddess into their repertoire, particularly when they feel they are not getting due respect. In fact, Goddess behavior is what your mother probably meant when she advised you to play hard to get. Sirens don't doubt they are special, even without the men who tell them so. But sometimes Goddesses feel that men need to be reminded of exactly how valuable that prize is. For the doyenne of the Goddess Sirens, look to Eva Perón.

Evita Perón

(née Maria Eva Duarte)

1919–1952

"There was a woman of fragile appearance, but with a strong voice, with long blonde hair, falling loose to her back and fevered eyes," wrote a smitten Juan Perón, a colonel with rock-star appeal in the Argentinean military. "She said her name was Eva Duarte, that she acted on the radio, and that she wanted to help the people . . . I was quite subdued by the force of her voice and her look."

Never mind that Eva Duarte was ridiculed by radio listeners for her country accent and that her "blonde" hair was actually pitch black when Perón met her in 1944. He remembered quite another Eva in his memoirs. You could say that he had been blinded by love, but oddly, Evita affected many people as if she'd come in on a white horse. Pale, humorless, and uneducated, she used the only capital she had at her disposal—an uncanny ability to seem heaven-sent.

Eva Duarte's story is, of course, legendary—the stuff of a Broadway musical and a movie. Eva's unlikely rise ends up sounding something like a fable in which she's both Robin Hood and the Wicked Witch. Born out of wedlock, she crawled out of ignominious poverty in the Argentinean outback. Within a decade of her arrival in Buenos Aires, she had catapulted herself from a virtual prostitute to B-minus actress to the mistress of Juan Perón, Argentina's Labor Minister—and then almost single-handedly orchestrated the coup that made him president. If you multiply Jackie O's appeal times four, you can calculate the power of the cult of Evita, Argentina's eternal First Lady. Years after her death from ovarian cancer at age thirty-three, Argentina tried to have their Goddess resurrected as a saint.

Some say Evita slept her way to the top, and so she did, using her assorted, carefully chosen sugar daddies to boost her career. But if sex were all it took, any number of women might have taken her place. So what was that magic dust she sprinkled in their eyes? It's hard, really, to separate the seduction of her lovers from that of the public, whom she called her beloved *descamisados* (literally, shirt-less ones). Indeed, her methods were the same. On the object of her affections she lavished a near religious devotion—a winning position in a country of devout Catholics—while creating the impression she'd stepped out of the clouds herself. That fragile appearance underscored the dramatic role. "Life has real value when one surrenders oneself to an ideal . . ." she claimed in a speech, cranking up the mike. "I am fanatically for Perón and the *descamisados*." About Perón she keened, "He is a god to us. He is our sun, our air, our water, our life."

For her devotion, the martyr was swiftly promoted to Goddess—or, come to think of it, maybe it was she who promoted herself. From her opulent office in the heart of Buenos Aires, the bejeweled First Lady held near papal audiences, emp-tying coffers of the rich to grant the wishes of the poor. Men actually knelt in the dust to spell out her name in flowers for her to walk on. Her picture was a staple in the working-class home. In her lofty language, her gilded look, and carefully orchestrated gestures, Evita created the perception that she was on a mission from God—and most believed she was.

Evita's Surefire Lessons for the Aspiring Goddess

Luckily, you don't need to land a small Latin country to be a Goddess, although the skill set involved in staging a *coup d'etat* might be useful. Perhaps Evita's short and brutish life might not be the one to emulate, but there's no denying that Argentina's first lady had something to teach us about holding men in thrall, while always keeping them at arm's length. At the core of that power was her abil-ity to transform herself into the distant stuff of dreams—wiles that work just as well today. Here's how she did it:

My beloved descamisados ... my, what a lot of chest hair.

Lesson One: Take the Higher Road

It was from the higher reaches of Buenos Aires that Evita was able to cast her image in stone. Citing Eva's success, a deposed president of Ecuador said, "Give me a balcony in every town and I'll win their hearts." She knew the power of literally rising above the crowd. The Goddess Siren seeks to keep a physical, as well as psychological, upper hand. You have a distinct advantage if you're taller than average; if not, you might start looking for higher ground. You may have noticed that Goddess-types perch on the arm of a chair or lean casually against the edge of a desk, rather than sit, and take whatever stage might be available in the room—anything to keep themselves floating above the fray. When they do step down to mix with mortals, the event seems remarkable—like the Princess who's decided to mix with her subjects for the day.

Wear those five-inch heels and your hair piled high. Build a balcony, find a staircase to descend, or make your home on a hill. Try anything short of a cherry picker to give you a lift. The idea is to give them a crick in their necks from looking up. Always remember to stand tall. Even the most diminutive Goddess will establish her regal presence if she throws her shoulders back and keeps her chin up.

11 THINGS EVITA WOULDN'T BE CAUGHT DEAD DOING

1) Wearing sensible shoes.

2) Getting sloppy drunk.

3) Letting her roots go.

4) Beginning a sentence with "Sit, I'll get that . . . "

5) Spilling her guts.

6) Hanging out at Off-Track Betting.

7) Deep discount shopping.

8) Housework.

9) Cracking a joke.

10) Telling the unadulterated truth.

11) Refusing to stand on ceremony.

Lesson Two: Create an Aura of Uncertainty

No one ever quite knew what side of the bed Evita would roll out on, and those girlish mood swings kept everyone on their toes. On the morning of her audience with Pope Pius XII, staff were more concerned about waking the mercurial First Lady than about keeping his eminence waiting. Hell had no fury like the First Lady scorned. With Evita, you might be banished to Uruguay or receive a spiffy new home by the end of the day.

So you may want to follow Eva Perón's example in moderation, but all Goddesses lay claim to, shall we say, emotional range. They'll purr when their men are expecting a roar and roar occasionally without reason. The boys are oddly impressed by the woman from whom they can't imagine what to expect. The idea is to inspire a teeny bit of awe and uncertainty without becoming a monster. Men want to feel you are a bit of a challenge—not impossible—to please.

Cancel a dinner date on a wisp of an excuse. Adore caviar today, and abhor it next month. Don't answer your phone for a week because you need to "think" about things. Then baffle them with abundant gifts and lavish compliments. Be aware that a miscalculated mood could come off like an aggravated case of PMS, which is not so winning. The successful Goddess always knows to pull back before she's gone too far. She never comes off as anything less than a woman of charmingly high—if indefinable—standards.

Lesson Three: Overdress for Success

"Not exactly a *descamisada*, eh?" said Juan Perón with a wink, referring to Evita's closets full of designer clothes. On a trip to Europe in 1947, she took her hairdresser and dressmaker—as well as sixty-four outfits and a "magnificent" selection of jewelry. In the midst of summer, she thought nothing of wearing a floor-length mink coat slung over her shoulders. Advised to take it down a notch, she articulated her philosophy. "Look, they want to see me beautiful. They all have their dreams about me and I don't want to let them down."

Clearly, the Goddess Siren doesn't have to wear a crown, but her look should definitely say "queenly." The secret is in the details. Always wear a little something that says, "I spent a million bucks"—or at least avoid saying, "such a bargain, I got four." Black pearls, say, or a touch of ermine at the collar. When the invitation says casual, make sure you're not.

Rely on dresses (unless you have impossibly long legs) to give you that exalted look. Fabrics should say luxury, not hot-water washable. Choose the more dignified de la Renta, Valentino, and Chanel—or their ilk—rather than the trampier Versace or Dolce & Gabbana. With jeans, wear that $1,000 top.

Lesson Four: Choose Your Words Carefully

No sooner did Evita rise to power than the records of her mongrel birth mysteriously disappeared, and officially sanctioned accounts of her early years began to read like a myth: "Like Venus, . . . Eva Perón was born from the sea." In her autobiography, *The Purpose of My Life*, she omitted dates and details from her childhood, and she always used lofty language in reference to herself. Sometimes, the Goddess Siren would dream about the way it might have been rather than face what was. As they say, "It's never too late—in fiction or in life—to revise."

As a Siren Goddess, it's not that you tell anything less than the truth, it's that you don't dwell on the truth that would take some explaining. If it comes up, cast it in your own special Siren light. Jobless? No, my dear, between opportunities. Held on drug charges a decade ago? A wild and crazy experiment in spiritual growth. Divorced more times than you care to count? All you can say is, you're of a passionate nature; you've always leapt before you looked. The Goddess Siren prefers to turn her image into a little spun gold.

YOU MIGHT BE INTERESTED TO KNOW THAT EVITA . . .

+ Threw Perón's mistress out of his house once she decided he was hers.
+ Scheduled a breast enlargement but never showed up.
+ Played the Sirens Catherine the Great, Elizabeth I, and Sarah Bernhardt in a series of radio plays.
+ Always wore her signature jewel-encrusted orchid pin, measuring 7-by-5 inches.
+ Was received by the Pope with all the honors usually afforded a queen.
+ Was so carefully embalmed that her dead body, kidnapped by Perón's opposition, was perfectly preserved when it turned up sixteen years later.

As hard as it is to do these days, the Goddess avoids coarse language. Try experimenting with statements that sound slightly regal or adopt the accent of actresses from old movies. "Would you take out the f-ing trash?" might become, "Could I prevail upon you to dispose of the garbage?" You're never having sex, by the way, you're in the "throes of passion." It takes twice as long, but you'll get the added mileage.

Lesson Five: Develop an Air of Quiet Mystery

Evita had no talent for conversation but where the Goddess Siren is concerned, often the less said, the better. Her unexpected silences make others a tad nervous and eager to please. When the Goddess wants the attention of the men in the room, she's more likely to fall silent than to jabber, and soon they're all dying to know what's on her mind. Two other Goddess Sirens—Greta Garbo and Jackie O—practically built careers on it. Jackie didn't talk exactly, she whispered.

By keeping her own counsel, the Goddess leaves a lot to the imagination and sets herself above a clamoring crowd too eager to tell all. Are there weightier matters on her mind, or does she simply want to be alone? She'll never tell.

The Goddess Siren is adept at keeping her admirers yearning for more, and those famous silences boost the effect. At times, she can be maddeningly sparing with the reassuring word or gesture. Was that good for you, he asks? Oh, I suppose, she says distractedly, leaving him wondering where it all went wrong. By withholding the goods, the Goddess Siren is one of those rare women that can turn a man obsessive.

POP QUIZ: ARE YOU A GODDESS SIREN?

Do you have the potential to be a Goddess Siren? Consider the questions below. If you answer "yes" to eight or more, you're on your way.

+ Do others seem overly concerned by how things will affect you?
+ Do clubs, teams, or other group activities leave you cold?
+ Are you very particular about your tastes—for example, do you always reject the first restaurant table or hotel room?
+ Are you moody or mercurial?
+ Do men tend to treat you as if you are fragile or in need of protection?
+ Are you more comfortable with silence than other people?
+ Is being waited on your idea of heaven?
+ Are you decidedly not "one of the boys"?
+ Do you like being in control?
+ Do you like being alone?
+ Do you see yourself as very different from other people?
+ Do you enjoy dressing to the hilt?

the companion

She was a cheerleader in high school, the party girl in college, and now she's probably the formidable woman behind some successful man. The Companion is his buddy, his champion, and the girl who's always ready to laugh with him. If she is always spotting the diamond in the rough, her secret is simple: in her eyes, every man *is* a diamond in the rough. When it comes to love, she falls hard and fast, and makes the best of the bumps along the way.

In her heyday, my mother was a Companion Siren—the first and last word on the corporate wife. And, indeed, my father never made a move without consulting his oracle. She was his politically savvy guru. My mother had a dead-on sense of the spectacular deal, as well as the catastrophe in the making. Legions of admirers felt the same way. On wintry weekend afternoons, I'd find her holed up in the den with a gentleman caller, chilled martinis close at hand. Ever the happy conspirator, my mother leaned into conversation—strategizing and laughing for hours on end. Was there anything "going on," as they say? My guess is no, in spite of the occasional feverish glance I saw directed her way.

The Companion Siren is assuredly sexy, but she's primarily his friend. With a twinkle in her eye, she shakes her head fondly at his hapless domestic ways, and stays up late with him when he has a yen for backgammon or gin. If she takes up his passions more easily than most, it's because, like a chameleon, she can change her color, and then switch back again. Her currency is empathy. It's how she forges that all-important intimacy for which she's known. To men confounded by the vagaries of the opposite sex, the Companion is a welcome relief. She's a woman who will grease his wheels, rather than set up tripwires in an emotional minefield.

For lessons in love, the aspiring Companion Siren needs to look no further than to the inimitable Jennie Jerome, the mother of Winston Churchill.

Lady Randolph Churchill

(née Jennie Jerome)

1854–1921

"If I were married to her whom I have told you about," wrote a besotted Randolph Churchill to his father, the Duke of Marlborough, "if I had a companion, such as she would be, to take an interest in one's prospects and career . . . I think I might become . . . all and perhaps more than you had ever wished and hoped for me."

Talk about love at first sight. When he wrote this letter, Churchill had met raven-haired Jennie, an American, just days before at a yachting party off the Isle of Wight. The two were thunderstruck—she by his potential, and he by her spirit and what she saw in him. Her hunch was dead-on. Over their twenty-year marriage, Randolph rose from an unlikely member of Parliament to Chancellor of the Exchequer, and might have become Prime Minister if cathouse syphilis had not turned his mind to Gruyère. She wrote his early speeches, organized political societies and rallies, and saw to it that they kept company with prime ministers and kings.

Brooklyn-born Jeanette Jerome was the daughter of Clara Hall and her husband, Leonard Jerome, a one-time lawyer and diplomat turned "King of Wall Street." Leonard loved women and music, usually simultaneously. He named his favorite daughter for the opera diva Jenny Lind before Clara got the drift. Putting an ocean between herself and her husband, Clara settled her daughters in Paris during the Second Empire, and then London—where young Jennie's American vitality caught on like a brush fire. Dubbed a "Professional Beauty" by the press, she was tracked just as a celebrity is today. After juggling an assortment of aristocrats, she chose Randolph at the tender age of nineteen.

She appeared "to be of another texture to those around her, radiant, translucent, intense," wrote statesman Lord d'Abernon, in a description that captures

Jennie's Siren appeal. She wore "a diamond in her hair, her favorite ornament—its luster dimmed by the flashing glory of her eyes." There was "more of the panther than the woman in her look," he continued, "but with a cultivation unknown to the jungle. . . . Her delight in life, the genuine wish that she should share her joyous faith in it, made her the center of a devoted circle."

Randolph's political cronies were all half in love with her, sending her affectionate notes and gifts—and Jennie added her admirers to her vast stable of friends, calling on them to further her husband's career. "And tell me, my dear, what office did you get for Randolph?" asked a miffed Prince of Wales (King Edward VII, later), on noticing her attentions to Benjamin Disraeli, then Prime Minister. "I am sitting next to _____, when I *might* be sitting next to you," wrote Arthur Balfour, signing his note, "Your miserable servant."

In Jennie, men recognized something of their own drive, but with a critical difference: she was able to keep up with them—riding hard to the hounds, gambling with abandon, and following the transactions of Parliament from as close a position as a lady was allowed. But she relished the role of back-office player. Ever the Companion, she didn't compete. By nightfall, she was furled in satins, tantalizingly feminine, and ready to engage with men over dinner with intelligent questions and witty banter. She never dominated conversation, according to her niece, but was "past master at the art of starting up subjects" for men to talk at her disposal. When "Jennie departed, she seemed to have left her mark on every room."

Our heroine was phenomenally accomplished in her own right—she founded and edited a literary magazine and penned plays and best-selling memoirs. But her most prized creations were her men. After Randolph's death, she was married twice again, to George Cornwallis-West and Montagu Porch—boy toys half her age, whom she molded into men. She took a special interest in her eldest son, Winston, helping him to rise in Parliament. "Winston she completely understood," wrote her niece. "Hot-headed ambition, the thirst for fame. . . ." She bragged she'd live to be eighty, but Jennie died, Siren-style, at sixty-seven from complications after toppling off her Italian high heels.

"To be happy in life, you need someone to love, something to do, and something to look forward to."

—*Lady Randolph Churchill*

Jennie Churchill's Formula for the Aspiring Companion

As the Companion Siren sees it, she has the best of both worlds—participating in his success without having to put up with the pressures. Along the way, she never lacks for friends or amorous attention. How does she walk the line? Note how Jennie managed in five easy lessons.

Lesson One: Mine His Virtues

When Jennie met young Randolph in 1873, he was the blossoming Roger Clinton of the Victorian era—unemployed, rarely sober, and riding on the family reputation. Plus, as Jennie's sisters were eager to point out, he had "poppy" eyes, an affected lisp, and a mustache that would pass for a ferret on his upper lip. Finally, as the second son of the Duke of Marlborough, poor old Randolph didn't even have a decent income. His prospects were considered dim. *"Next!"* you say? Not so for Jennie. She sat out the dancing on the Lido deck, as Randolph had "noticeable problems matching his feet to the intricate figures of the quadrille" (read: bad dancer). He's clever, she thought, taking measure of his biting wit. Ding. He thinks I'm cute, which shows uncommonly good taste. Ding. Ding. And he's titled. Ding. Ding. Ding. And she had a secret premonition of his brilliant future. Where others saw problems, Jennie saw a heap o' potential.

Not that the aspiring Companion Siren suffers fools. At least not gladly. But in her profound appreciation of men, she focuses on the plus side of the slate. "Treat your friends"—and your men—"as you do your best pictures," Jennie said, "and place them in their best light." Note his fine mind, instead of his inability to write a coherent letter. While he may eat like a savage, perhaps he's adroit at the thoughtful gesture. So, as the Companion, you proudly talk up his talents wherever you go. So persuaded is the Companion of his incipient genius that she is his kingmaker—the woman without whom he knows he would be only half as good.

Lesson Two: Share His Passions

Take note that Jennie devoted "an hour or more . . . to the reading of the newspapers" and she devoured Gibbon's voluminous treatise on Rome at her beloved's suggestion. If you move among gladiators, our Siren might say, don't go throwing up your hands because you don't get his whole obsession with killing lions. The Companion sharpens the spears, makes a few helpful observations about the reigning Emperor, and subscribes to *Impalement Monthly*.

That's not to say you won't pursue your life's agenda—only that you understand what he's into. Don't just ask, "Honey, how goes it on the floor of the exchange?" Read the financial pages and develop your own investment strategy. If he's a whiz with car engines, find out what a carburetor is. The guy knits? Ball his yarn—with very little on, of course. If men bond by doing, reasons the Companion, why can't women jump into the game? What better way to become one with him?

10 THINGS JENNIE WOULDN'T BE CAUGHT DEAD DOING

1) Starting a sentence with "the problem with you is . . ."
2) Seeing the glass half empty.
3) Welshing on a gambling debt.
4) Playing the sympathy card.
5) Missing a party.
6) Kicking him out of bed for snoring.
7) Failing to rise to the challenge.
8) Leaving people out of the conversation.
9) Holing up alone for the weekend.
10) Complaining that she's bored.

Lesson Three: Let Him Shine

A man "is not inclined to feel very tenderly toward a girl who has just beaten him on his own ground at lawn-tennis or golf," noted Jennie. Not that our Jennie necessarily "let men win," as my own mother (the Companion) strongly advised me as I set out with my racquet (no contest, in my case). With disarming charm, Jennie cast herself as the attractive bumbler—so she never came off like the triple threat she could easily have been. She was master of the self-effacing joke.

On her foray into portrait painting, at which she was astonishingly successful, Jennie described her works as "martyrizing many models." She reported in a letter that her first picture in oils was "mistaken by an admiring friend for a brilliant piece of wool-work!" Collecting on a paltry gambling win, she cracked, "someone will now want to marry me for my money."

Instead of looking for kudos, the Companion Siren tells the opportune joke at her own expense—or chalks up her success to luck or a particularly good day. She throws her game, if she must. It's not that important to her; she'd rather make his day and keep the peace. Her natural inclination is to share the spotlight. She thinks it's more fun that way.

Lesson Four: Make Lemonade
(Out of Lemons)

Marriage to Randolph was no happily-ever-after proposition, with his syphilitic mood swings, long sojourns abroad, and, okay, a possible interest in young men. Just when the path began to look a little clear, he'd go and spoil it all by doing something stupid like challenging a Royal to a duel—which would mean lying low in Ireland for the year. "Life is not always what one wants it to be," Jennie wrote, "but to make the best of it as it is is the only way of being happy." Instead of whining about Ireland's gloomy weather, she'd entertain herself by concocting a dinner party—then she'd serve up some hot-button issue as a conversational dish. Was Jennie ever discouraged? Well, maybe just a little. But shopping or taking a ride through the moors would restore her faith. "No outing with Jennie could be dull," said an admirer. "Her gray eyes sparkled with the joy of living."

Handed the difficult situation, the Companion turns the sow's ear into a Kate Spade purse—making it a blast for herself and everyone else. And when her team's down, the Companion gets those pom poms up in the air. The Companion turns a power outage into a séance, a failed meal into a chance to try a new restaurant, and a faux pas into a funny, self-deprecating tale. A little *joie* goes a long, long way. Her enthusiasm has sex appeal.

Lesson Five: Make Yourself Available

The Goddess tantalizes by staying just out of reach. The Competitor makes her conquest and walks away. But with the Companion, what you see is what you get: the sooner, the better. She wants men to know she's there for them and that she won't be playing games of hide-and-seek.

In and out of marriage, between husbands, at twenty and sixty-two, Jennie had countless male admirers, and never as a result of playing hard to get. There was not a coy bone in her body. When she loved (not infrequently), she was on the next train. During a weekend house party, she tracked down George Cornwallis-West in the hunting field when she became impatient for his return. She traveled up the Nile to throw herself into "Beauty" Ramsden's arms. She tiptoed out the back door in the night to lock lips with the dashing Count Kinsky. She was betrothed to Randolph within three days. Too easy, you say? So thought most of fashionable London, but what did Jennie care? She had her amours eating out of the palm of her hand.

Stalking is not the strategy, by the way—*Fatal Attraction* was never the inspirational tale. But if the Companion wins him by being his champion, she's not likely to pull away suddenly—unless, of course, he's mistreating her. She has the unshakeable confidence of a Siren, and so assumes he wants her all. She's not put off by the down-to-the-wire invitation, unless she's otherwise engaged. The afternoon flight to Paris? Her passport's ready. To that dinner at 11 p.m., she says, who would have it any other way?

YOU MIGHT BE INTERESTED TO KNOW THAT JENNIE...

✦ Had a fashionable tattoo of a snake twined around her left wrist.

✦ Claimed to be part Iroquois.

✦ Always used pink-tinted light bulbs when entertaining so her guests would be bathed in a flattering glow.

✦ Thought it was in bad taste to use explicit language while telling an off-color story (of which she told plenty).

✦ Apparently tried to heed her mother's advice: "Never scold a man, my dears. If you do he will only go where he is not scolded."

✦ Is responsible for the "Manhattan" cocktail, which she commissioned for the election of Samuel J. Tilden as New York Governor in 1874.

POP QUIZ: ARE YOU A COMPANION SIREN?

You know you're a good friend—but are you a Companion Siren? Consider the questions below. If you answer "yes" to eight or more, congratulations! You're Companion material.

✦ Are you a team player?

✦ Do you see men as wonderful playmates?

✦ Would you call yourself spontaneous?

✦ Are you an organizer?

✦ Are you more of an extrovert than an introvert?

✦ Are you more comfortable in the company of men than women?

✦ Are you an optimist?

✦ Do you hate to miss a party?

✦ Are you considered trustworthy?

✦ Are you a keen judge of character?

✦ Do you like to "juggle men"—that is, maintain relationships with a number of them (not necessarily romantic)?

✦ Do you crave intimacy?

the sex kitten

*I*f sex is always on his mind, then it will come as no surprise that the Sex Kitten is his fantasy. And when she's in the room, other dames stand not a ghost of a chance. She is the universal pinup girl, mainlining lust to his brain—the proverbial luscious and forbidden fruit that begs to be picked. The Sex Kitten is the archetypal "good" girl who promises naughty pleasures in the bedroom, without actually saying the words. She can be a bit of a tease.

My college roommate, Paula, had not a distinctive feature in her sweet basset hound face, and flaunted what would kindly have been called generous hips. Yet without the advantages of beauty, she was a true Sex Kitten—proving that such talents are not just skin deep. Paula had a ripe, sexual openness that men couldn't seem to resist, along with a ditzy, baby-doll demeanor that brought out the protector in them. Each admirer saw her through his own lens. To one she was a muse, inspiring a series of ghastly medieval-style paintings. Another was convinced she would someday give birth to his brood of kids. In truth, Paula was pre-med, with ambitions of pursuing podiatry in that seemingly addled head.

Herein lies the rub: the Sex Kitten's talent to arouse is so powerful, it drives all rational thought from a man's head. Her "innocence" sparks his desire to leave a protective imprint; she provokes the Pygmalion that lies within. But the Sex Kitten risks becoming a cliché or a caricature—the vast, blank canvas on which he paints his elaborate fairy tale. Use her lessons sparingly, like a dab of scent behind the ears. And remember that the Sex Kitten's talents, if not tempered, don't always age well. Who else but Marilyn could be our role model?

CASE STUDY:

Marilyn Monroe

(née Norma Jean Baker)

1926–1962

"She had a luminous quality," said a friend after her death, "a combination of wistfulness, radiance, yearning, that set her apart and yet made everyone wish to be a part of it, to share in the childlike naiveté."

Ah, Marilyn. Born Norma Jean Baker to a mentally disturbed mother and a father she never met, Marilyn was shuttled between foster homes, eager for love that nobody gave. She might easily have faded into obscurity if that hourglass figure had not emerged at thirteen. Suddenly, delightfully, the world "opened up," she later recalled. In her search for love, the transformed Marilyn made the most of her bounty. She bared her midriff, wore her sweaters too tight, and strolled the California beaches swiveling those trademarked hips. "She realized what she had, and she didn't mind showing it off," said James Dougherty, the factory worker she married at sixteen to avoid a new foster home.

Marilyn's rise in pictures was more of a struggle than you might think. There were countless bit parts, studio contracts dropped, and the "nudie" photos that nearly destroyed her career. "I earned fifty dollars that I needed very bad. That wasn't a terrible thing to do, was it?" asked the shrewd "victim," about the pictures that ended up in *Playboy*. Charmed by her candor, the public forgave her. In comedic films like *Some Like It Hot*, *How to Marry a Millionaire*, and *Gentlemen Prefer Blondes*, she defined the American bombshell, freely advertising her sexual wares with the innocence of a cherub. "She was half child," said Clark Gable, "but not the half that shows." Beginning with *Scudda-Hoo! Scudda-Hay!* and ending with *The Misfits*, Marilyn made twenty-nine films, racking up more box office and fan mail than Hollywood had ever seen before.

Those who loved her never recovered. Married to Marilyn for only nine months, baseball great Joe DiMaggio carried a torch, weeping openly at her funeral and sending flowers to her gravesite every week. Playwright Arthur Miller poured the details of their strange union into scripts. Her adoring public hangs on to their iconic memories: Marilyn in *The Seven Year Itch*, standing over a subway grate, her white skirt blowing up in the air. Marilyn singing "Happy Birthday" in a breathless baby voice to an American president. Countless posters immortalizing her platinum tresses and parted lips. Will we ever know for sure if her affair with JFK was the beginning of the end? Will the conspiracy theories ever cease?

Grable and Harlow came before her. Dozens of celluloid Sex Kittens have come since. But what was it that made Marilyn like no one else? With a roll of her shoulders and that break-out smile, she promised men sex without strings, stamped with a Good Housekeeping Seal of Approval. A study in contrasts, she was helpless, yet sexually aggressive; childlike and maternal; dumb, but shrewdly aware of her effect—and something more. "She had a talent to make people feel sorry for her," said one of her photographers. That vulnerability spawned a national desire to protect her.

"I don't mind living in a man's world as long as I can be a woman in it."

—*Marilyn Monroe*

Marilyn Monroe's Tasty Tips for the Aspiring Sex Kitten

"Die young and leave a beautiful corpse," said James Dean, and surely Marilyn did at age thirty-six. While the Sex Kitten peaks in youth, her charms can be moderated and used with age.

Lesson One: Ask for Directions

While men would rather get hopelessly lost than ask for directions, scientific studies show they'll happily show a woman the way—a tip Marilyn picked up early in the Sex Kitten game. She developed a wide and revolving network of men on whose advice she depended for her every move. Should she make this film, buy that house, wear these clothes? What books should she read to look smarter and informed? "She was like a lost little kitten," said one observer. *Exactly.* A little Sex Kitten. No man seemed to be able to resist the thrill of playing Marilyn's Svengali, even as she sought permission just to get out of bed. But in our brave new world, that kind of abject dependence might cost you more than you're willing to pay. Still, the aspiring Sex Kitten—even one with a Ph.D. and a seven- figure salary—loses nothing by asking a man for a little guidance now and then. It doesn't really matter if he knows that she's perfectly capable. He's happy to suspend disbelief. Leave him with the impression that you're safely tucked beneath his wing.

You note he was particularly "forceful" and "visionary" in his presentation for the Board of Directors—you'd like his help in putting together a "little talk" for the company retreat. And since he clearly works out, might he recommend a gym? He's as likely to view this behavior with suspicion as you would be to turn down an expensive gift. You'll find that there's no such thing as a silly question, and the high-flown compliment will strike him merely as deserved praise.

Warning: This strategy may cause dizziness or nausea if used daily.

Lesson Two: Put Some Wiggle in Your Walk

Marilyn started with a little wiggle in her walk, but she honed it into high art on the set of the film *Niagara*. In a scene shot from a distance, her high heels threw her off on the cobblestone street, creating the undulations she was known for. The walk, 116 feet of film, was the longest in cinema history, and caused such a sensation that Marilyn adopted it from then on.

Okay, you've spent years getting down that no-nonsense walk—the one that signals would-be muggers and workplace harassers that you mean business. But now you have a Siren agenda. Short of cobblestone streets in your area? Don't let that stop you. Spend a weekend in the country in your five-inch heels. As you're making your adorable way over rough terrain to pitch a tent or chop kindling, concentrate on keeping your gait loose and fluid. As always, practice makes perfect. Soon you'll be swiveling your hips with the best of them.

11 THINGS MARILYN WOULDN'T BE CAUGHT DEAD DOING

1) Balancing her checkbook.
2) Wearing sweats in public.
3) Burning her bra.
4) Leaving home without lipstick and perfume.
5) Getting anywhere on time.
6) Taking offense at a blonde joke.
7) Developing OCD.
8) Trying not to look sexy.
9) Looking for love in all the right places.
10) Beginning a conversation with, "Studies show that . . ."
11) Leaving her phone off the hook.

Lesson Three: *Wear It Tight and White*

Between childlike innocence and knowing lady of the evening, the Sex Kitten strikes a precarious balance—losing her footing when she descends into day-old tramp. More often than not, Marilyn wore white, branding the indelible image of a shimmering sex angel. In those wholesome fifties-style duds, you might find the solution, as Marilyn did. Bring polka dots, peek-a-boo ruffles, cinched waists, push-up bras, and flirty skirts back into the mix.

Everything about your wardrobe should say squeaky clean, even if you're sporting a leather bustier and chains. Remember, you're the gal who makes sin sweet. Imagine June Cleaver on the way to a nooner with Ward, or Britney Spears headed off to summer camp. It's always a smidge too tight, and an inch too short, and shows a provocative expanse of skin. As for lingerie, it's feminine and expensive, unless you've "forgotten" to wear any at all.

"Before marriage, a girl has to make love to a man to hold him. After marriage, she has to hold him to make love to him."

—*Marilyn Monroe*

Lesson Four: Tell Your Sad, Sad Story (Optional)

Marilyn's tale of foster homes, a mentally ill mother, and lustful relatives was always potent, though it came out differently in each retelling. Even in small ways, Marilyn played the Little Nell lashed to the proverbial railroad tracks. Either she "hadn't eaten since yesterday" or she was "exhausted" by the demands of her career and fans. I'm bearing up as well as can be expected—her delivery seemed to say—but, golly, I sure hope help gets here soon.

By her sad, sad tale, the Sex Kitten aims to inspire the possibility of rescue—bringing out the heroic fireman in every man. (Hey, doesn't every little boy want to be one?) It helps, of course, if you have a tale to tell. Dredge up those epic struggles in which you were young and naive, abandoned, or things spun way out of control. For inspiration, look at the classic stories that fuel literature or the tried and true fairy tale. But shelve those stories about lovers who did you wrong. Why remind him of who came before?

Lesson Five: Look Perpetually Ready for Sex

Marilyn's first husband described her as an insatiable nymphet with a dangerous appetite for roadside sex. On that subject, Marilyn sounded a little more conflicted. Still, there's no denying that our Siren looked as if she had just gotten out of bed, or would soon join a threesome between the sheets. The Kitten needs to imply sexual promise, even if she doesn't act on it. She's perpetually ready to squeeze.

Always squeaky clean, perfumed, and provocatively dressed, the aspiring Sex Kitten still never looks too carefully "put together." The sprayed helmet of hair and starched collar only bring to mind the dictatorial nun or asylum nurse. A little disarray enhances the image of sexual openness. But the clincher, of course, is in the eloquent phrasing of her body language.

The Sex Kitten leans into her man and purls back her shoulders, shifting slightly from hip to hip. Absently adjust your clothes and brush your fingers across your chest or lips. Frequent and gentle touch is key. Apply soft pressure to his elbow or forearm. Coax a stray hair back behind his ear. When dancing, make it cheek to cheek. Touch, touch, touch. There's no substitute for the electric power of skin on skin.

YOU MIGHT ALSO BE INTERESTED TO KNOW THAT MARILYN...

+ Dreamt repeatedly of appearing naked in church.
+ Underwent plastic surgery to correct a bump in her nose.
+ Earned more money for Twentieth Century Fox than any other star by 1953.
+ Worked out with barbells.
+ Was incapable of getting anywhere on time or getting a scene on the first take.
+ Was hand-sewn into her clothes sometimes, they were so tight.
+ Maintained, on occasion, that champagne and caviar were her favorite foods.
+ "Became a symbol of the eternal feminine," for the entire world, it was noted at her funeral.

Lesson Six: Perfect the Wardrobe Malfunction

Janet Jackson runs a poor second to Marilyn, who gave us the greatest wardrobe malfunction in entertainment history: in *The Seven Year Itch*, the skirt of her silky white halter dress collided with an updraft from a subway grate, exposing her panties. But on camera and off, Marilyn was an expert. She might rig a strap to snap, and then scramble for a safety pin to prolong the pandemonium. Or simply dispense with the undergarments to give the boys an unexpected lift.

There's no cheaper thrill for a man than when a woman's attire goes askew, exposing uncharted bodily territory. The slit skirt, the slippery shoulder strap, and the descending neckline all have infinite potential—though you'd do well to avoid pants so tight they threaten to expose your posterior. If you dare, try a week without underwiring and pour yourself into fitted shirts. Throw caution to the wind by discreetly slipping your panties into your purse. When you're the happy victim of a sudden shift, remember to express surprise and a dash of girlish embarrassment. A show of modesty is critical.

POP QUIZ: ARE YOU A SEX KITTEN SIREN?

She's the tastiest of bon bons. Do you have the Sex Kitten's cream filling? Say "yes" to eight or more of the questions below, and you could be a bona fide Marilyn.

+ Do you tend to resort to a show of helplessness to get out of a tight spot?
+ Does it make you feel powerful when men think of you in overtly sexual terms?
+ Do you consider Jane Fonda in *Barbarella* a more interesting role model than Condoleezza Rice?
+ Do you feel pampered when men run the show?
+ Are you proud of your femininity?
+ Do you like to draw attention to yourself?
+ Do you feel frumpy if you're not showing skin?
+ Around you, do men tend to play Pygmalion?
+ Did you have an unhappy childhood?
+ In your love relationships, are you looking for Daddy?
+ Are you sometimes viewed as clueless or innocent?
+ Would you consider losing your make-up case/toiletry kit a crisis?

the competitor

Growing up, she was the tomboy, the girl for whom "dress" was a dirty word. Forget Barbie. Our Competitor preferred to play with her brothers—building tree forts, riding dirt bikes, and devising new ways to blow things up. Did that all change at age thirteen? Not for the Competitor Siren. She's never happier than when she's operating on the hardscrabble playing fields populated by men and fearlessly breaking rules. She has the soul of the hunter-gatherer, softened by the seductive lines of a dame.

You think she's a myth? Meet Samantha, the only female fly fishing guide on the East End of Long Island. Her reputation for heartbreak is legend, though a little baffling at first. Sure, she's tall, fair, and attractive in an all-American way. But—yikes—don't those dirty fingernails make them shudder? And what kind of Siren wears clothes that she fell asleep in the night before? Yet Samantha never fails to command male attention in whatever room she saunters into. Passionate about her sport, she is a better angler than most men, and seems also to share their taste for the neat scotch and the ribald tale.

Men are intrigued by the Competitor's independence and her apparent lack of need for them, though it's more of an illusion than the real thing. Under that persuasive mask of indifference, she's as reliant on their company as she is on her need to come in first. He admires her courage, her competence, even the ice-water that sometimes runs through her veins. She's low maintenance and thrillingly high risk. In the Competitor Siren, he finds his passionate soul mate and adventuring equal. On his fantasy sail around the world, the Competitor Siren's on the sheet.

Adventurer Beryl Markham conquered a world dominated by men and stole their hearts along with it. For the aspiring Competitor Siren, her lessons in love are a good place to start.

CASE STUDY:

Beryl Markham

(née Clutterbuck)

1902–1986

She was "generally felt to be Circe . . . but not your run-of-the-mill Circe. Imagine casting a spell over Ulysses so she could go along on the journey, learn navigation, see the world," wrote Martha Gellhorn in a preface to Beryl Markham's memoir, *West with the Night*. "[S]he bewitched his company of men so that they did not resent her intrusion in their macho society, but welcomed her."

West with the Night described Markham's solo flight, east-to-west, over the Atlantic, a trip made on a dare in 1936. Hers was the first successful "water-jump"—a challenge deemed greater than Lindbergh's west-to-east journey, due to the treacherous headwinds. As Markham slid into the cockpit, her soignée white flying suit fluttering in the breeze, international headlines trumpeted "BEAUTY TO FLY TODAY." Well-wishers bid Beryl what they knew was her last farewell. Nearly twenty-two hours later, winging it without a radio, she crashed on Nova Scotia, 300 feet short of the water's edge. "I'm Mrs. Markham," she said, by way of a cordial hello, nonplussed by the blood gushing from her head. "I've just flown from England."

You'd be hard pressed to find a Competitor like Beryl Clutterbuck today—let alone the unusual circumstances that created her. Her family emigrated from England to Kenya, where Beryl was virtually deserted. Her father barely paused from his farm work, and her mother soon returned to England, leaving her young daughter behind. Beryl quickly became fluent in Swahili and ran with the Masai, who thought of her as more boy than girl. She learned to run, jump, and hunt—and to endure excessive pain without a whimper. She developed an "Amazon-like capacity" for emotional control. "She beat me with a *kiboko* until I was raw and bleeding, but I became more defiant," she wrote of a governess, charged with taming the child savage. Dragged by a horse for seven miles, she barely thought to mention it, except to pity the horse.

"If your hunch proves a good one, you were inspired; if it proves bad, you are guilty of yielding to thoughtless impulse."

—*Beryl Markham*

At a certain point, it's hard to say whether Beryl aspired to join the men's club, or whether they struggled to keep up with her—so handily did she outstrip them on their own turf. The first woman horse trainer in Kenya, she brought a host of winning thoroughbreds to racing circles. As a bush pilot, she routinely risked her own life in the line of rescue. Of her memoirs, that bastion of masculinity Ernest Hemingway said, "She has written so well, and marvelously well, that I was completely ashamed of myself as a writer." She was the sexual aggressor. According to an onlooker, she "liked nothing better than to creep barefoot into the bedroom of her choice at the end of a day's work."

Over men, Beryl exerted a powerful "psychological charisma." She was forced into marriage at age sixteen, to a thirty-two-year-old man who fell in love with her on sight. She kept the name of her second husband, a wealthy aristocrat named Mansfield Markham, but left him after a handful of years. Journalist Raoul Schumacher clocked in as husband number three (on and off) for nearly twenty years. Throughout her marriages, her indiscretions were so legion that one lover kept count by the number of nails he pounded into his door. Once men were bagged and bedded, she quickly tired of them. She felt the need for fresh conquest. Only the glamorous white hunter Denys Finch Hatton eluded her net, which naturally made her crave him all the more.

In Beryl, men fell in love with a mirror image—or was it the man they aspired to be? Her "delicious recklessness" and passion for the game were the quicksand into which they fell. The ride was never run-of-the-mill or dull. That casual ability to reverse the gender roles was absolute; they were the ones who suffered, rarely did she. Into her eighth decade, still a Siren, Beryl was beating a hasty retreat to the door.

Beryl Markham's Lessons for the Competitor Siren's Walk

If you're a rule-breaker or a daredevil who's still deeply female, you could be a budding Competitor Siren. Learn how through Beryl Markham's example.

Lesson One: Flirt with Adventure

We've spent millennia building civilized nations, and women pride themselves on taming their men, we know. But in the Competitor Siren, he hears the call of the wild—a deep connection to his aboriginal self. The Competitor may not be the marrying kind, nor the girl he imagines bringing home to Mom (Dad might be another story). Yet he finds it hard to resist a woman whose spirit and passion are equal to his manliest self.

From earliest childhood, Beryl viewed herself as one of the boys, but wanted to do more than just compete in a man's world. She soloed across the Atlantic on a trip that had taken the lives of many who had tried before. In horse racing circles, she captured the East African Derby, Kenya's top race, five times. For all we know, she probably peed standing up. Our Competitor Siren was addicted to action and risk, which, for her, was an erotic thrill. She succeeded in realms that test the manliest of men.

As an aspiring Competitor Siren, look for the life challenge or physical adventure and strive to be the best at your chosen "sport." Your actions should speak loudly and for themselves. If your field of play is the boardroom, gamble on the new product or the inspired acquisition. Be the entrepreneur and a free thinker. The sporting Competitor climbs K2, shoots skeet, or hunts down bonefish in the

Seychelles, while never thinking about fatigue or risk, only the thrill. As a Competitor Siren, you would rather fail in the spectacular attempt than succeed by being corporate or dull. Your passion for living has an allure all its own.

Lesson Two: Cross Dress

"She wore trousers with men's shirts and audaciously left the top button undone," or in the style of the white hunter, tied a silk scarf "rakishly at her throat." Even without a mount, Markham effected jodhpurs and boots in the modish style of the Hollywood director. Her mannish glamour wasn't just a question of throwing on the rumpled wad left lying on the floor. It was carefully, if quickly, orchestrated. It was no accident that in her silky white overalls, Beryl made her water jump departure look like a fashion runway walk.

Sure, you can high-style it in a gown and heels when the occasion demands, but your Siren self truly comes out when you borrow his threads. The way you put it together, Orvis and Brooks Brothers look like they were designed with a delicious purpose. Accessorize a tuxedo with Victoria's Secret—or wear waders with a bustier and g-string. Don a cop's uniform when you want to present a more arresting image of yourself. In your jeans, his necktie makes a dandy belt.

What is it about a woman in men's clothes that titillates? It's a popular tease in countless Hollywood flicks. Is it that he's thinking about your body where his once was? Or maybe that devil-may-care, thrown-together look leaves the impression that it slides off as quickly as it slipped on. However it works, aim for slim lines with a show of skin. You look delectable, yet capable, with a sexy spin.

Lesson Three: Be Low Maintenance

Refreshingly, the Competitor Siren never demands those special attentions that baffle men—the sensitivity to her feelings or elaborate recognition of holidays. PDA makes her slightly ill. She never takes the temperature of a relationship, and she'd rather get a good night's sleep than talk an issue to death. If something really bothers her, she goes for the jugular or keeps her thoughts to herself.

Our Siren pared down her life to Spartan needs. Had she had her way, said a friend, "she would have had a place she could have cleaned with a hose." As it was, Beryl kept it to little more than a bed, a chair, a trunk, and his aftershave. Her disregard for material things kept her ready for adventure, set to go at a moment's notice. And so it followed that the drop dead glamour came without makeup and hours of fuss. Beryl's ineffable style had more to do with her attitude than anything manufactured or bought.

As an aspiring Competitor Siren, you require less maintenance on all fronts. Aim to be more streamlined, less precious, and not quite so obsessed with your emotional outlook. Spend less time at the vanity table—forget the mascara, the collagen, and that infernal hairdryer and straightening brush. On a weekend trip, pack for two nights—he'll be shocked and deeply impressed.

---

10 THINGS BERYL WOULDN'T BE CAUGHT DEAD DOING

1) Asking for a do-over.
2) Ordering a wine spritzer.
3) Reading *He's Just Not That Into You.*
4) Registering for a china pattern.
5) Wallowing in regret.
6) Spending the evening with Häagen-Dazs and chick flicks.
7) Feigning a headache to get out of sex.
8) Beginning a sentence with, "My therapist says . . . ."
9) Overdressing.
10) Lying in bed all day.

Lesson Four: Approach Sex Like a Man

In the mood for a little lovin', Beryl set the Victrola to a Glenn Miller tune. It was her shy way of saying she was ready for a little action. And then the "idea (of sex) was born . . . happened . . . and was over without fuss." Sounds kind of familiar, doesn't it? Her technique was "startling and erotic," and remarkably without the usual complications and strings. She never demanded added value, never used tricks. Beryl presumed that mutual sexual satisfaction was a reward in itself. More than one lover went on record to say he'd never had it so good.

For Beryl, sex was spontaneous, "a pleasurable form of exercise, like dancing, with as many changes of partner." She never understood it as a tacit contract, the way many women do. As an aspiring Competitor Siren, you'll cast aside the double standard that gives him the upper hand. Don't expect candlelight dinners or a wedding band. Your passion is equal to his. Take a thousand lovers, and do it without guilt. If he captures your fancy, invite him up to see your etchings. You might keep him for an hour, fall in love, or turn him loose the next day. Don't sit around waiting for *his* call. Move on to the next. Like our role model, Beryl, be proud of your body. Waste no time in getting out of your clothes.

Lesson Five: Never Let Them See You Sweat

"It seemed impossible to me to cry from physical pain as a child," Markham wrote—a trait she learned from Masai warriors. That "Mona Lisa face" would frustrate, baffle, and intrigue. Was she shy, made of stone, or did she just not give a good goddamn? "She was a good brave girl, all guts and a heart of gold," claimed a lover. But about romance she was singularly unsentimental. Men "longed to disturb that millpond calm," wrote a biographer, who claimed that Markham's inscrutability was key to her irresistible appeal.

It's not that the Competitor Siren doesn't feel. In fact, her loyalties often run true and deep. But somewhere along the line she picked up the caveat: A display of emotion is for sissies, little girls, and geeks. "With Beryl, men did all the flirting," reported one of her frustrated lovers. Her approach was almost bored, with a hint of irony.

The aspiring Competitor Siren would rather draw blood by biting the inside of her cheek than look overeager. And when a man has let her down, she'll greet this disappointment with stoic indifference. Demand nothing, and he'll rush in to fill the void. Watch for the surprising reversal in roles. Passionate declarations, even tears, will be his from now on, not yours.

YOU MIGHT ALSO BE INTERESTED TO KNOW THAT BERYL...

+ Hurled a spear with deadly accuracy, like a Masai warrior.
+ Swore that she would have "nothing to do with women . . . EVER," after a governess beat her.
+ Caused a scandal by having affairs with the Duke of Windsor (then still Prince of Wales), and his younger brother Prince Henry, at the same time.
+ Seduced white hunter Denys Finch Hatton away from *Out of Africa* author Karen Blixen (Isak Dinesen).
+ Claimed that her pilot's log book was "more precious than any diary."
+ Copied the same gabardine slacks by the dozens in every color through a shop that catered to Frank Sinatra, Bing Crosby, and Gene Kelly.

POP QUIZ: ARE YOU A COMPETITOR SIREN?

Wondering if you're a Competitor Siren? If you answer "yes" to eight or more questions, you may well be. If not, you can always use some of the Competitor's tips.

+ Do you generally feel more comfortable with men than women?
+ Have you always been highly competitive?
+ Do you have a higher than average libido?
+ Are you usually unaffected by what others think?
+ Do you get a thrill out of risky situations or breaking rules?
+ Does it take a lot to make you cry?
+ Have you always preferred boys' toys to girls' toys?
+ Do you work in what is traditionally considered a man's world?
+ Would you rather spend the day learning a new sport than at a spa getting a makeover?
+ Are you impatient with self-analysis?

the mother

It's long been fashionable to devalue the domestic dame, but in our heart of hearts we know her talents are deeply alluring to men. He's built to crave the Mother from cradle to grave. I think of her as the stealth Siren: the woman who's not necessarily perceived as a threat until she's lured your man away. Wrapped in her metaphorical womb, don't kid yourself, he'll gladly forfeit the challenges of the new-fangled womanly ways. The Mother Siren makes him feel coddled and protected in a harsh world.

My grandmother fits in decidedly here as a Mother Siren. Even in her plump dotage, she had irresistible appeal to men everywhere she went. On visits with us, she was keyed into my Dad—actually bringing him wind-up toys that made him laugh, along with the imported caviar treats he craved. Around Grandmum, my father's rough edges seemed to melt away—which perhaps explained why my grandmother, twice widowed, was never without a man. Her third and last husband was a dashing life-long bachelor entering late middle age. "How did you do it?" I asked, marveling at her ability to get apparently any man to heel. "I make them feel comfortable," she said. Come again?

The Mother Siren attends to a man's inner child and gives him the nurturing that others foolishly presume he's outgrown. She's a stickler for creature comforts—cheerful surroundings, square meals, and clean clothes, even if it's not she who's slaving over the ironing board. She's a godsend at the sickbed, in crisis, and particularly, in his hour of need. By pampering the child within, the Mother revives a devoted man. Here's the kicker: in the bedroom, the Mother has a wicked ability to please. Nothing is too kinky—or creepy—to raise a hair on her head.

You'll often find the Mother Siren in the seemingly plain Jane, who slips off her glasses to reveal a world-class seductress. Beware! She could be your sister, cousin, or your best friend. As Mother Sirens go, the Duchess of Windsor was the crème de la crème.

Wallis, Duchess of Windsor

(née Bessie Wallis Warfield)

1896–1986

"I have found it impossible to carry the heavy burden of responsibility and to discharge my duties as King, as I wish to do, without the help and support of the woman I love," said King Edward VIII in 1936, on giving up the British throne. The woman in question was, of course, the American "Mrs. Simpson," infamously married to a second husband and divorced from a first. The Prince's devotion to Wallis would become "the romance of the century," and has been the subject of gossip and speculation since. How did she do it, and did they live happily ever after for the rest of their lives?

Bessie Wallis Warfield was born in Blue Ridge Summit, Pennsylvania, to Teackle Wallis, a failed businessman who made Alice Warfield a young widow. To Alice's great shame, she was forced to muddle by on earnings from running a Baltimore boarding house—though a rich uncle paid for Wallis's splashy society debut. As a child, Wallis had "the most entrancing glance out of the corner of her eye." Later, she developed wit, a knack for lively conversation, and a voracious eye for pretty clothes. She was never "silly" around boys, reported an admirer. "By her earnest attention . . . she made us feel that we were really a rather gifted group of youngsters."

In the galaxy of Sirens, Wallis Warfield was surely one of the unlikeliest—described by photographer Cecil Beaton as "attractively ugly, *une belle laide*." Yet she was steeped in beaus from early on. She had the "gift of making you feel that you are the very person she has been waiting all her life to meet." In love, she somehow missed the boldface writing on the wall. At twenty, while visiting cousins in Pensacola, she met Lieutenant Earl Winfield Spencer, a Navy pilot whom she quickly married, thinking he was "a man you could rely on in a tight place." It turned out he was a raging drunk instead. With their marriage on the

rocks, she followed him to Hong Kong. He dragged Wallis by the hair on visits to brothels, an experience that came in handy later on (see Lesson Two).

After she divorced, Wallis weighed her options. She "must have had thirty proposals," reported a suitor, before she settled on Ernest Simpson, an American who took her to London. She scaled British society as a hostess *extraordinaire*.

"A woman can't be too rich or too thin."

—Wallis, Duchess of Windsor

"I'm afraid the Prince is going to be lonely," said his mistress, Lady Thelma Furness, before embarking on an extended trip. She asked her friend Wallis to check in occasionally. No problem there. The Mother Siren laid on her most solicitous attentions—playing HRH's hostess and organizing his day. The Prince, now utterly relaxed, did his needlepoint and her toenails, provoking his butler to quit. The cuckolded Mr. Simpson, went the joke, was penning a play— *The Unimportance of Being Ernest.*

Their blithe romance came to an end when King George died, and the new king refused to keep Wallis sidelined as a mere mistress. "Without her I have been a very lonely man. With her I shall have a home," he wrote in an address that the Prime Minister wouldn't permit on the airwaves. He sought "to be protected and guided . . . and to establish . . . the one thing he had never known," wrote a biographer, "—a happy family life." Was it worth their lifelong exile in France? "She had given me loving care" and "devotion," said the Duke, which he claimed "to have cherished above all else."

Wallis Warfield Simpson's Recipe for
the Aspiring Mother Siren

Read up on Pamela Harriman and Camilla Parker-Bowles, who also chose the Mother Siren route. Pamela befriended and studied Wallis as she made her way up in the world. Here's what the aspiring Mother Siren should know:

Lesson One: Divine His Innermost Needs

A favorite with the gals in his youth, the handsome Prince (a.k.a. David, King Edward VIII, and the Duke of Windsor) had a mistress and several spares when he met the divorcée from Baltimore. But while others were dazzled by his title and the goodies it conferred, shrewd Wallis looked deeply into his troubled soul. She treated him as "a man first, as a Prince second," according to one of his equerries—and in so doing, blew the competition directly out of the fishing hole.

"I have given my husband every ounce of my affection," she later wrote, "something he never had a great deal of in his bachelor life. Notice, I use the word affection. . . . It means doing the things that uphold a man's confidence in himself, creating an atmosphere of warmth and interest, of taking his mind off his worries."

Be he an emperor, king, or chief exec, the Mother Siren sees him as the flesh-and-blood man he really is. To her, he's barely out of high-tops and short pants, at least where his emotional needs are concerned. She responds to his boyish desires with maternal interest. "Wallis, you're the only woman who's ever been interested in my job," said the Prince, wistfully. After spending a rough day among his subjects, the Prince knew his Wallis would not only be eager to hear about the ups and downs of the royal wave, but willing to massage the aching monarchal wrist. The Mother is his confidante, sounding board, and hospital nurse—all solicitous attention and soothing words.

As an aspiring Siren, you'll develop that famous maternal sixth sense—listening not just to his words, but to what he may have failed to say he needs. Is he tired, stressed, perhaps looking for diversion? Bar the door, take the phone off the hook, and get busy booking a Tahitian holiday or a week in Vail, even if you don't have a clue how to ski. When he's down, do that mean imitation he loves of his dippy sister—or gather his friends for a poker game or casual supper. If he's soaring, crack the champagne and hire the orchestra. Poor baby, he's doing time for embezzlement? Get busy shoveling dinners into Tupperware.

"Forgive me for not writing but this man is exhausting."

—*Wallis, Duchess of Windsor*

10 THINGS WALLIS WOULDN'T BE CAUGHT DEAD DOING

1) Cracking her gum.
2) Beginning a sentence with "Yo, David . . . "
3) Quoting Betty Friedan.
4) Playing Twister.
5) Leaving dirty dishes in the sink.
6) Stocking up on TV dinners.
7) Wearing day-old lingerie.
8) Tying one on.
9) Bungee jumping.
10) Gossiping about the Duke's sexual proclivities.

Lesson Two: Be a Kinky, Sexy Mama

The royals were none too keen on the less-than-virginal Mrs. Simpson, so they assigned intelligence agents to dig up the dirt. The rumor mill alleged variously that she was a prostitute, a hermaphrodite, a man, and a dominatrix. However, the famed "China Dossier" may be where we should look for the truth. The dossier described the Asian-style sexual techniques Wallis mastered on her whirlwind tour with her first husband through the brothels of Hong Kong. Of

particular interest was the so-called "Chinese grip," in which a woman contracts her vaginal walls to "an extraordinary degree." She employed the technique to help the over-excitable (and modestly endowed) Duke to sustain, it was said, until the Duchess was ready to receive.

There's more. A punishing governess apparently instilled in the Prince a taste for masochistic thrills—and the Duchess, it was rumored, picked up where the nursery left off. Though, drat, nobody knows what exactly went on behind the closed Windsor doors. Where is that tell-all book? "That Wallis Simpson provoked in him profound sexual excitement is self-evident," wrote a biographer. "That such excitement may have had some kind of sadomasochistic trimmings is possible, even likely." Wallis knew how to release the Prince from his inhibitions and the "idiotic self-consciousness and shyness" he often felt.

It follows that the Siren who attends to a man's innermost needs would know how to say night-night with a little twist. The Mother never blanches when he wants to act on fantasies that seem a little quirky. You'll answer to Helga, Herr Gruber, or Mother Superior, if you get my drift. Consider keeping a reference library for "special" films and books (*Kamasutra* works)—perhaps a closet for costumes and props. He'll be a slave for your favors and a devotee of your sexual gifts.

Lesson Three: Rein Him In

When Lady Thelma Furness returned from the U.S. to resume her affair with the Prince, he was ice cold, and more than chummy with her friend Wallis. At dinner, the Prince reached for a lettuce leaf with his fingers, and Wallis playfully slapped his hand, telling him to mind his manners. "I knew then that she had looked after him exceedingly well," said Furness, who quietly departed the house party the next morning, down one Prince.

Wallis's mother-nanny act startled observers, but "this treatment," claimed a biographer, "was no more than David himself wished." Wallis had added the magic ingredient: her criticism appeared to be "based on love" and a fervent desire to help him "be at his best." Wallis acted on what Mother Sirens instinctively know: unruly boys will test the limits. But they positively thrill to the confident woman who is willing to draw the line when they've gone too far. I know these men intimately, and when you stop to think about it, so do you.

The Mother Siren has a pronounced sense of what's right and wrong. The focus isn't character but the traditional domestic realm. Here she rules, no questions asked. She operates out of genuine conviction, not (necessarily) a burning desire to control. Still, the aspiring Mother Siren should strive not to make scolding an extreme sport. Use the subtle Southern reprimand: "When you eat, bless your heart, I find myself wondering if that fork actually gets in the way."

Lesson Four: Run the Show

Hostessing, landscape design, holiday plans, house parties—you name it, the Duchess put Martha to shame on the home front, and the Prince's reliance on his beloved's advice and management of their domestic lives "created a deeper bond." The morning after their wedding, Wallis woke to find David, the Duke of Windsor, at her bedside. "And now what shall we do?" he asked. How the mighty do fall to the Mother Siren's directorial skills.

It's the oldest story in the book. He leaves his long-suffering wife for his secretary or assistant. But ask yourself this: has that secretary ever been described as an organizational ditz? Trust me, she's a whiz and a Mother Siren working overtime. Under her vigilant eye, the man who once made his own coffee suddenly has no idea where the percolator is and gets confused making restaurant reservations or dialing directory assistance.

The Mother Siren knows exactly how to make things supremely easy for the "boss." In fact, he wonders how he muddled through before she came along. As a Mother Siren in training, you'll see to it that he never crosses paths with the dry-cleaner or an overdue bill. For whatever ails him, you've got the remedy in the medicine chest. Run a tight ship, so the captain can navigate more easily.

YOU MIGHT ALSO BE INTERESTED TO KNOW THAT WALLIS...

+ Used diminutives like "little" and "baby" in addressing her husband.

+ Laundered her loose change and pressed her paper bills.

+ Was repeatedly named one of the world's best-dressed women.

+ Weighed herself every morning to keep rail thin.

+ According to reports, was secretly sleeping with an irresistibly handsome car salesman called Guy Trundle while she was keeping company with the Prince.

+ Was received by the British royal family only twice—at the Duke's death and at hers.

Lesson Five: Make a Home

"There are not many women who can pick up the keys of a rented house . . . and make it look as if a family of cheerful good taste had been living there for two or three centuries." But Wallis Simpson, in the words of writer Rebecca West, was surely one of them. She raised homemaking to an art form with this simple philosophy: "a place where good things out of the past would intermingle gracefully with good things of the present, with the accent on color and a pleasing symmetry." Her homes were miniature kingdoms where her Duke reigned.

Create settings in which your gentleman callers feel comfortable. Out go the spindly antiques on which visitors are afraid to settle; in come the overstuffed furniture, pile rugs, and soothing chintz. For her man-in-residence, the Duchess duplicated the spirit of the rooms he loved from his childhood in hues of chocolate, scarlet, cream, and gold—and mixed in photos, paintings, trophies, trunks, books, and souvenirs. Don't underestimate the power of a vase with fresh flowers—Wallis didn't. And remember, nothing says failed Mother Siren like a bathroom that's growing mold.

When the Duke opened the fridge, he could rely on a constant supply of his favorites—stewed fruit, baked apples, and rice pudding. If the way to a man's heart is through his stomach, mainline your love with food.

POP QUIZ: ARE YOU A MOTHER SIREN?

What kind of Siren lies within? The following questions will help you identify your hidden potential. Answer "yes" to eight or more, and you're Mother Siren material.

✦ Do you strive to make men feel comfortable rather than challenged?

✦ Is the home your bailiwick?

✦ Do you think men sometimes have peculiar sexual needs but it's better not to make too much of it?

✦ Do you think men have the raw deal?

✦ Is Laura Bush more interesting to you than Hillary Clinton?

✦ Are you a problem solver or a fixer?

✦ When you travel, do you pack for every contingency?

✦ Do you believe that the way to a man's heart really is through his stomach?

✦ When you meet a man, do you usually try to imagine what he might have been like as a little boy?

✦ Do you think discipline and order are important?

✦ Do you like the feeling of being relied on?

✦ Are you calm in a crisis?

a word on archetypes

The sooner the aspiring Siren understands her archetype, the more easily she can begin to deploy her irresistibility to full effect. But remember, just because you fall predominantly under one archetype doesn't mean you can't borrow lessons from another. The Mother Siren might divine his innermost needs—as outlined on page 62—and at the same time take up the Companion's mantle and share his passions. Pamela Harriman, a clear and dangerously present Mother Siren, was a stellar example. Sirens often straddle archetypes, dominating in one while employing the characteristics of another. The Mother/Companion, the Competitor/Goddess, and the Sex Kitten/Mother combinations are not uncommon.

A caveat: know the source of your power. Don't add raisins to your martini, or you'll ruin the taste. The elusive Goddess Siren, for example, must be careful not to diminish her power by being available in the way a Companion is. The source of the Goddess's appeal is her mystery, the ineffable aura that she cannot quite be attained. The Companion's power lies in her talent for creating intimacy. If the two can be combined, it must be carefully calibrated. The actress Sarah Bernhardt worked both ends beautifully.

Beyond archetype, there are myriad ways in which a Siren makes herself irresistible—through her conversation, humor, chic, even her divine cooking skills. In upcoming chapters, aspiring Sirens can learn by example and veteran seductresses can pick up a few tips. You'll see how the great Sirens worked from archetype, while giving seduction their signature twist. What made Cleopatra unforgettable, for instance? How did Catherine the Great conquer them in the bedroom? Why is Susan Sarandon the thinking man's fantasy? Their secrets are unveiled here.

PART TWO

Personalizing Your Appeal

Be Unforgettable

Sirens whose legends survive centuries have left their indelible mark on the men of their time, sometimes even altering the course of history through their gravitational pull. But what of those who live among us—say, a fabulous seductress such as yourself? In your own sphere, can you be as memorable as Cleopatra was to Rome? Like anything, it takes work. A Siren is not a Siren unless she finds her own way to stand out from the crowd.

Who are the outrageously unforgettable Sirens? The list stretches back to Eve, and winds up with Sirens like Nicole Kidman and Angelina Jolie. What makes these women unforgettable could be the sum of their parts or that *thang* thing they do so well. Sometimes their talent for being unforgettable is hard to describe. Taking a look through our microscope, we can find a few invaluable tricks of the trade that our famous Sirens have passed on. Through careful dissection, their lessons can become your talents. Give them your own inimitable spin. A Siren is an original through and through.

In the pages that follow, you'll find women who have made being memorable a high art. Their very names have enduring cachet to Sirens in the know. The Queen of Kings, Cleopatra made the world's most unforgettable entrance on a barge up the Nile. Josephine Baker, a self-styled exotic, bucked the tide of her times and made black forever beautiful. Lola Montez was the scandal that ruined a king, and Garbo was Garbo because she was so damned eccentric. And because of Coco Chanel, your scent will linger forever in his mind. Learn from them all, one lesson at a time.

find your signature scent

Coco Chanel

(née Gabrielle Bonheur Chanel)

1883–1971

Competitor/Goddess Siren

"It's an unseen, unforgettable, ultimate fashion accessory. It heralds your arrival and prolongs your departure," said the matchless fashionista, Coco Chanel. She wasn't talking about silk stockings, the clutch, or high-heeled shoes. My dear, she meant perfume. Coco was the first designer to mix her own potion and add her name, making Chanel No. 5 the world's first branded scent. It was designed to evoke "eternal woman," the one who lingered in his mind long after she'd left the room. Marilyn Monroe purred she wore nothing but Chanel to bed. *Vogue* noted that it drove men gaga. "Husbands, beaus, taxi drivers—*everybody* loves it," everywhere. Since then, nothing has said *seductress* quite like perfume. In the words of Chanel, "no elegance is possible without it . . . perfume is part of you."

Gabrielle Bonheur Chanel was the mother of reinvention—or perhaps a Siren with a Goddess's knack for spin. She would change the story of her humble, semi-orphaned childhood often, into something a little less *Les Misérables*. During a brief, uninspired career as a chanteuse, she took the name Coco. She stumbled over her talent for chic quite by accident. On the way to the horse races, she hacked the front out of a jersey she didn't want to pull over her head. Coco added "a ribbon, a collar, and a well-placed knot," and she sold ten like it that very day.

"My dear, my fortune is built on that old jersey that I'd put on because it was cold in Deauville," she claimed. From her first millinery shop in Paris, financed by her lovers, she threw out corsets and bobbed her hair. She introduced the "little black dress," sportswear, costume jewelry, and the garçon (little boy) look. If she succeeded in putting irresistible in a perfume bottle in 1923, it's because she instinctively knew the ingredients. "I'm not pretty," she confessed to a lover. "No, you're not," he admitted, "but I know of no one more beautiful than you." Now, there's a backhanded compliment a woman can endure.

Coco had a horror of being dependent on a man. She also famously believed that a woman "not loved is a woman lost." Men were invariably smitten by the force of her personality. She was "small and fascinating," remembered a friend, "something like the idea of Cleopatra that Caesar loved." She was direct and witty in conversation and a deeply attentive listener. After leading everyone to believe she could be seduced, Coco would simply disappear. Her approach to men and sex was disarmingly casual. The Duke of Westminster was one of many driven to bended knee by her charms. "There are many duchesses," the elusive Siren said, turning him down, "but only one Coco Chanel." We can only hope that hearing it in French cushioned the blow.

Coco's lovers included a millionaire cavalry officer, a polo king, a hothouse poet, the composer Stravinsky, and a Nazi occupier of Paris who would make the French question her loyalty. Like many Competitors, she was proud of her attraction to many, more than a commitment to anyone. But if into her life true love did fall, it was for the rakish "Boy" Capel, who married a young heiress before returning to Coco. After he died in a fiery car crash, Coco never fully recovered. "We were made for each other," she said, but as a cool Competitor, she never let her grief show.

In her dotage, Coco brought out Chanel No. 19, and market-tested it on herself. She told reporters she'd been stopped in the street by a man asking where her unforgettable scent came from. "A woman can be beautiful at twenty, charming at forty, and irresistible all her life," she claimed. A Siren's best accessory is her signature fragrance.

Coco's Lesson

As a child, Coco had been taught to scrub herself whistle-clean with lye soap, and thereafter loathed the smell of "female body odors." All her life, she was blessed and cursed with a sensitive nose. She threw herself into making her own fragrance like a zealot, demanding things that had never been done before. "I don't want hints of rose, of lilies of the valley," she said, referring to the fashionable perfumes. "On a woman, a natural flower scent smells artificial. Perhaps a natural perfume must be created artificially." By mixing the extracts of Spanish jasmine with benzyl acetate, Chanel created a potion that wouldn't fade within moments of putting

it on. It would be the world's most expensive scent, but its wearer would be unforgettable. She chose the fifth of eight samples—hence, Chanel No. 5.

Chanel No. 5 may remind him of his first love or his mother's vanity table. For me, it summons up the glamorous image of my Cousin Georgie. Georgie lived in Paris, but sashayed through my childhood eons ago. Tall, mysteriously dark, and perennially fur-coated, she lived a life of exotic abandon to which I was never privy, but which I imagined was surely scented by the Chanel she left behind in every room. Today, if I pick up the tiniest whiff of Chanel, Georgie is all but standing there.

SCENT SUGGESTIONS FOR THE SIREN

Arpege *(Lanvin)*	Lovely *(Sarah Jessica Parker)*
Beyond Paradise *(Estée Lauder)*	Mitsouko *(Guerlain)*
Chanel *(5, 19, 22, Coco, Cristalle, Allure)*	My Sin *(Lanvin)*
Chloe *(Lagerfeld)*	Opium *(Yves Saint Laurent)*
CK One Electric	Shalimar *(Lanvin)*
Eau d'Hermès	Splash-Ivy *(Marc Jacobs)*
Fabu *(Dana)*	Trésor *(Lancôme)*
Femme *(Rochas)*	White Shoulders *(Evyan)*
Fracas *(Piguet)*	Youth Dew *(Estée Lauder)*
Joy *(Patou)*	

Chanel No. 5, Marc Jacobs, Lancôme's Trésor . . . it's not so much what you choose, but that you make your decision carefully. Fragrance speaks. Bold or subtle, spicy or sweet—what scent tells the world most eloquently who you are? Choose a scent that spins your legend faithfully. Your perfume should make you the Siren he never forgets—not the woman who changes with the fashions of the month. Tonight, he's moved by your scent on his pillow, but your fragrance will bring you back long after you've packed your bags and absconded with another man.

No dashing into Saks between appointments—in fact, why not fly to Paris and do your research? Consult the experts in five-star perfumeries. Begin with a few descriptives of your essential personality, along with the smells that intrigue you most. When you've narrowed it down to some scents you like, try a few on. Do you feel like your Siren self or some trampy imposter who's wearing your clothes? In enclosed spaces, would you like to make your acquaintance or a quick exit?

"A woman wearing no perfume has no future."

—*Paul Valery*

"Smells are surer than sights and sounds to make your heart-strings crack," claimed Rudyard Kipling. Look for rheumy eyes from the men in your life when you spritz that scent. When the right one comes along, you'll surely know.

DAB IT, DON'T OVERDO IT

You've walked behind her on the sidewalk. She's overtaken you on the train. Her scent doesn't say unforgettable—no, it says she may have failed to bathe. There's nothing that can kill the effect of the sweet Siren like too much perfume. You shouldn't smell submerged, but more like it's natural to you. Take Coco's advice and dab it wherever you want to be kissed. Spritz only after you've showered, not to cover up your work-out at the gym.

develop eccentricities

CASE STUDY:

Greta Garbo

(née Greta Lovisa Gustafson)

1905–1990

Goddess Siren

Long after Greta Garbo had dropped out of public sight, an old friend paid a call on her in her ivory tower apartment overlooking the East River in New York City. When Garbo left the room to fix him a drink, he spotted an odd little figure peering out from under the couch. "It was a troll," he found, on closer inspection. "You know those little plastic dwarves with the ugly, wild, magenta and turquoise Dynel hair?" Apparently, a whole community of them were lined up in formation—though he never broached the subject with Garbo of what exactly was going on. Yet, each time he returned to Garbo's apartment and checked, the trolls were marching in a different direction.

Hmmm. Trolls? Under the couch? And I thought stamp collecting was strange. It's another one of those riddles wrapped inside of a mystery called the "Swedish Sphinx." If ever a Goddess Siren ruled through mystery, it was the film icon Garbo. Arguably, she rules still. She created her aura with layer upon layer of eccentricity, defined by a single line when it was all said and done. "I vant to be let alone," she said to John Barrymore in the 1932 flick *Grand Hotel*, her luminous face expressing pain, hope, weariness, love, and—was that?—a dash of regret. Who was Garbo? She never made a move or uttered a word that gave a single clue.

Greta Lovisa Gustafson came to Hollywood in 1925 via Stockholm, Sweden, on the coattails of Mauritz Stiller, a "hot" director who faded from view. Stiller spotted the "haunting sensuality" in his plump protégé. She was gawky, shy, and almost plain then, but on film, the Siren came through. Aptly, he named her

Garbo—the rough equivalent of "spirit" in Swedish. "Look at that girl!" said studio head Louis B. Mayer, mesmerized by "the expression emanating from her eyes." She was immediately offered a contract. "He knew as sure as he was alive that he had found a sex symbol beyond his or anyone else's imagining," wrote actress Louise Brooks. And "no contemporary actress was ever again to be quite happy with herself."

Garbo's Hollywood reign lasted a mere fifteen years and twenty-five films—among the top faves were *Camille*, *Wild Orchids*, *Mata Hari*, *Anna Karenina*, and *Ninotchka*. She was the First Lady of the screen, starting in silent films and continuing through Garbo talkies. "Gimme a visky with chincher ale on the side—and don't be stinchy, baby," was her famous first line in *Anna Christie*. She was "every man's fantasy mistress"—*La Divine* to the French. "What, when drunk, one sees in other women, one sees in Garbo sober," said a critic. Jeez, couldn't other women catch a break?

"There is no one who would have me— I can't cook."

—*Greta Garbo*

"That face, what was it about that face?" asked the director Billy Wilder. "You could read all the secrets of a woman's soul." And there was her singular walk, that husky Swedish-accented voice, and those "thirsty" onscreen kisses that telegraphed passion that—let's face it—Garbo didn't feel. On a more conventional dame, the legend surely wouldn't have stuck, but it was Garbo's inexplicable behavior that fanned her eternal flame. She drove men to distraction with her eccentric elusiveness.

To a dinner invitation, it wasn't "No," or "Let me check," but "How do I know I'll be hungry that day?" A studio head was mystified to find the roses he sent to Garbo returned. She often referred to herself as an old man or a little boy (and we don't know to this day if her sexual preference was for women or men). And her need to be alone could take such peculiar turns: crossing the Atlantic, Garbo had her meals served privately—on deck every night aboard a different lifeboat. In tribute to two popular actresses of the time, actor Wayne Morris labeled his faucets Ann Sheridan and Greta Garbo, instead of Hot and Cold. Of the two, Garbo lives on.

Garbo left actor John Gilbert at the altar on his first desperate attempt to marry her. On his second try, the runaway bride climbed through a roadside washroom window to escape. Didn't it ever occur to her to say, politely, no? Though the details are sketchy, Aristotle Onassis, Cecil Beaton, actor George Brent, Erich Rothschild, author Erich Remarque, and conductor Leopold Stokowski were enchanted, some even obsessed. "She led us all on," wrote Beaton. "You wanted to put your head on her lap or bury your face between her breasts and have her kiss you." Into her mystery, each man saw his own redemption, if he could just figure out how to capture her. Artist Jackson Pollock claimed that he'd only fallen in love three times—once on passing Garbo in the street. He took off after her and wasn't seen again that day.

After *Two-Faced Woman* flopped, thirty-six-year-old Garbo retreated from view, but never into obscurity. Over the next fifty years, she traipsed in disguise on daily walks through New York City, while paparazzi waited at every corner to snap her pic. True to legend, Garbo wanted to be alone. She scurried back to an apartment filled with Renoirs, Bonnards, and, apparently, little trolls.

"The story of my life is about back entrances, side doors, secret elevators, and other ways of getting in and out of a place so that people won't bother me."

—*Greta Garbo*

Greta's Lesson

"She has the most inexplicable powers of fascination which she uses freely on all and sundry," said the writer James Pope-Hennessy about the hours he spent in England with Garbo. His start is promising, but here's the twist: "And then it gradually dawns on one that she is entirely uneducated, interested in theosophy, dieting and all other cranky subjects, has conversation so dull that you could scream." Bad news for Garbo, my friends, but hope for the Siren whose only obstacle to being unforgettable may be that she's painfully dull.

Do men nod off just as you arrive at mid-sentence? Are your interests limited to comparison shopping and sitcom reruns? Do your seductive charms suffer from that saucy smile that you've failed to coordinate with a rakish wink? Just kidding, girls. . . . Naturally, you're far more interesting than this. Still, it wouldn't hurt to develop a charming array of eccentricities, and you'll be the seductress that no one forgets.

Garbo rarely did anything that anyone could understand or predict—indeed, it was a large part of the secret of her phenomenal success. Even her rabid need for privacy was inconsistent. When she learned that her butler was taking cash from tourists to watch her skinny dip, did she fire him instantly? No, Garbo laughed uproariously instead!

"That so few now dare to be eccentric, marks the chief danger of our time."

—*John Stuart Mill*

The abrupt mood swing, the non sequitur, and the veil of secrecy work, as long as you use them strategically. It's reported that Garbo made breakfast a covert operation, and it could get a little old. You don't want to come off like a nervous rabbit with an uncontrollable tic. A Siren needs to be in command of her eccentricities, and pair them with a confident personality.

GO FOR SHOCK VALUE

Sometimes all a Siren needs to be memorable is a single quirk—but it should be a striking one. Nineteenth-century Siren/actress Sarah Bernhardt, for instance, took to sleeping in a rosewood coffin, so she could get accustomed to the idea of the inevitable. Countless postcards were sold in Europe and America of the "Divine Sarah" (who lived to be eighty-eight) reclining in her flower-strewn casket—an eccentricity that contributed to her unforgettable Siren legend as much as her long list of lovers did.

Develop a range of benign phobias. Collect andirons or listen to Gregorian chant. Bathe weekly in lemon juice or un-homogenized milk. Take up unicycling, cheese-rolling, or curling as your sport. Swim in the nude, even when you're not alone—or, like Garbo, disappear mid-sentence because you "vant" to be alone. When considering the cryptic, don't forget the ever-popular communing with the dead. It made Shirley MacLaine unforgettable, why not you? Or take to wearing a striking hat with a veil or reading with a lorgnette. Grow giant sunflowers in the garden and paint your walls electric blue.

Using Garbo as your muse, express your kooky self without reserve. You'll long be remembered for that adorably odd thing you do. Just make sure those eccentricities heighten the irresistible, not the disturbing. A house full of cats, for instance, says spinster—not Siren with feline appeal. Strive to be an interesting standout, not a slave to the creepy or weird.

make an indelible first impression

Cleopatra VII

69 BC–30 BC

Competitor Siren

"She came sailing up the river Cydnus in a barge with a poop of gold, its purple sails billowing in the wind, while her rowers caressed the water with oars of silver which dipped in time to the music of the flute, accompanied by pipes and lutes," wrote the ancient historian Plutarch, in his description of the notorious Cleopatra. Dressed as Aphrodite, Cleopatra reclined under a canopy of gold cloth, while on either side, boys costumed as Cupids cooled her with fans. An "indescribably rich" perfume wafted from the vessel to the riverbanks, and her most beautiful ladies-in-waiting were dressed as Graces and Nereids. By night-fall, hundreds of lights cascaded down from the roof of the barge in ingenious patterns, creating a "brilliant spectacle."

Cleopatra had been summoned to meet with Mark Antony, a general and statesman in the Roman Empire. Antony needed cash from Cleo to wage war with the unruly Parthians. As a Roman province, Egypt was obliged to ante up, but the ambitious Queen had her own agenda: to enlarge her beloved country's territory. To that end, it was noted, "no general ever planned an attack more brilliantly." She so dazzled Antony with her entrance that he became weak in the knees, and he never quite recovered his equilibrium. Over the next decade, he turned over land like a drunken Santa at Christmas—to Rome's permanent chagrin. It was the beginning of the end of one of history's greatest *femmes fatales*. The lovers were finally cornered by Roman armies in the Battle of Actium. Antony fell on his sword for his ladylove, who later poisoned herself with an asp. They were buried together in Alexandria—that is, the one on the Nile.

Age cannot wither her,

nor custom stale

Her infinite variety:

other women cloy

The appetites they feed,

but she makes hungry

Where most she satisfies:

for vilest things

become themselves in her.

—Shakespeare's *Antony and Cleopatra*

If ever a Siren lived large, it was Cleopatra. Descended from the Ptolemaic Dynasty of Alexander the Great, she was the People's Princess—the first Greek ruler even to bother learning the Egyptian language, along with Aramaic, Hebrew, and a smattering of Syriac. She was "imperious, determined, courageous, ambitious, intensely alive," wrote a biographer—and ruthless enough to slaughter her siblings to keep her throne. Her goal was to expand Egypt to the borders it had enjoyed in Alexander's glory days. To that end, she engaged all her resources, though it was, of course, her personal attractions that closed the deal. "Her own beauty, we are told, was not of that incomparable kind which instantly captivates the beholder," wrote Plutarch. Yet her presence was "irresistible." In spite of the hooked nose, there was "an attractiveness about her person, together with a force of character which pervaded her every word and action. . . . It was a delight merely to hear the sound of her voice."

When it came to men, Cleopatra seems to have excelled at leaving an indelible first impression, tailor-made to impress her prey. Antony was not the first powerful Roman to fall to her charms or to be manipulated. Some years before, Caesar passed through Egypt and found Cleopatra gone—banished by the court of her baby brother, Ptolemy XIII. To enlist Caesar's help, the Queen had herself smuggled through enemy lines rolled up in a carpet, which was dramatically unfurled before the astonished conqueror. Impressed by the Queen's brilliance, and taken with her charm, Caesar restored Cleopatra to her throne—and gave her Cyprus as a bonus prize. Little King Ptolemy, a kid still, ended up at the bottom of the Nile.

Need I tell you that Cleopatra was a Competitor? Or that men were swept away by a woman whose chutzpah equaled their own? For the love of their Egyptian Queen, both Caesar and Antony ended up dissing their wives, thumbing their noses at the Forum, and signing their death warrants. Had Caesar and Antony not dallied "overlong" in Alexandria, the world might look entirely different today. Cleopatra drove her lovers to ruin on the rocks of romance, and she had them both at "hello."

Cleopatra's Lesson

"She relied above all upon her physical presence and the spell and enchantment which it could create," wrote Plutarch. Like any Siren of substance, Cleopatra knew the first impression she made had to be indelible—in 41 BC, this was doubly so. Antony, Cleopatra, and Caesar were often forced to spend years apart, with-

out so much as an e-mail to keep in touch. She saw to it that her entrance was daz-zling, and the follow-up just as good. Knowing her Romans by reputation, she carefully planned the assault that would capture their hearts.

When Antony summoned the Queen to Tarsus, she bided her time to heighten his anticipation. She then turned down his invitation to dinner with one of her own. "Dearie," she said, or its Egyptian equivalent, "don't go to all that trouble. I'll just have cook throw together a little something on the boat." Imagine his awe as he headed down to the riverbanks and saw Cleopatra's sumptuous ret-inue. Her Aphrodite was intended to flatter the image he had of himself as the wine-god Dionysus—and word spread that these gods planned to revel for "the happiness" of their subjects. She knew Antony was a carouser and a "lover of women," with a weakness for exotic luxury, so Cleopatra fed him drink and a din-ner "magnificent beyond words." Noting Antony's "humor broad and gross," she got down and dirty herself, and treated him "without reserve." She finally handed over the furniture and tableware as party favors to his peeps. Antony was captivated by all her glamour; Cleopatra became his mistress, and he her slave.

With the more sophisticated Caesar, Cleopatra streamlined her approach. Her entrance in a carpet impressed the celebrated tactician on the battlefield and her coy charm bewitched. I don't mean to speak for Caesar, but as Cleopatra leapt out, he must have thought, "now here's a woman to be reckoned with." This twenty-one-year-old girl "rapidly captivated the experienced womanizer of fifty-two," noted a biographer.

Since the beginning of time, Sirens have been brilliant stage managers who orchestrate their arrivals for impact. Carole Lombard entered making them laugh. Josephine Baker held them off until they were positively salivating. Jackie O thrilled them with her spectacular wardrobe. Maybe you'll be more like Pamela Harriman, who made an unforgettable first impression with her listening skills. You might arrive in a Rolls, wrapped in a fur, or with a gorilla on your arm. You could make your indelible first impression by your clever opening line. Sometimes the simpler the approach, the more memorable—the legend lives on of the lady who simply dressed in red at the funeral of John Dillinger.

Like Cleopatra, assess the field, then come up with your game plan. The first impression is most important; you may never get a better chance to dazzle him. Your entrance might suit your whims, or reflect something you know about his personality. As a Siren, your entrance should never slip by unnoticed—unless it's through enemy lines rolled up in a rug. Employ the element of surprise, and invent new ways to say that an unforgettable Siren has just entered the room.

CONSIDER THE EXTRAVAGANT GESTURE

Ever the drama queen, Lady Emma Hamilton swooned on first meeting Admiral Horatio Nelson, who had just returned triumphant from the Battle of the Nile. Nelson was so taken with Emma, he fell instantly in love—as soon, of course, as she'd been revived. Nelson moved in with Lord and Lady Hamilton and carried on the affair right under Emma's husband's nose. But that's another crazy story and another Siren, who we'll save for another time.

create a scandal

Lola Montez

(née Eliza Gilbert)

1821–1861

Competitor Siren

Lola Montez pulled into Munich, Bavaria, in 1846, intent on booking her "Spanish dance" into one of the city's theaters. Her reputation for scandal had preceded her. Lovely Lola had been jailed in Berlin for whipping an officer across the face and then was ousted from the city. In Warsaw, she directed lewd gestures at her audience while they hissed. In St. Petersburg, Czar Nicholas I cut her to a single performance for fear of what she'd get up to next. Understandably, Munich's respectable theater owners barred their doors. Lola appealed to Bavaria's King Ludwig I. Casting his eyes over Lola, Ludwig asked whether her magnificent bosom was "nature or art." Obliging, she slashed open her bodice with scissors and was instantly booked as the halftime act for—ironically—*The Enchanted Prince.*

In her time, Lola Montez would become as famous—or infamous—as Queen Victoria, and as sought after as any Siren since Helen of Troy. She built her career on a talent for scandal that snowballed, and the greater the scandal, the deeper the line of men who collected outside the stage door. Her dance? A *tarantella*, of sorts. Lola stamped her feet vigorously to music while chasing an imaginary spider through the scanty folds of her costume. From London to Warsaw, audiences paid scalpers' prices and noisily disapproved. "I love you with my life, my eyes, my soul," wrote Ludwig, worried that Lola might fall for one of the gentlemen who "swarmed." He built her a castle and made her a Countess. She plunged him into an abyss of scandal that shot his monarchy to hell.

"Wouldn't it be a little crowded on the honeymoon? You and me and the hanging party?"

—*Lola Montez*

Lola Montez began life respectably in Limerick, Ireland, as Eliza Gilbert, the daughter of a soldier and a milliner's assistant. She spent most of her youth in India, where it was noted that the blue-eyed beauty was "volatile." Escaping an arranged marriage, Eliza eloped at age fifteen with a Lieutenant Thomas James—an unhappy arrangement she left after five years. Aboard a ship headed back to England, she compromised her reputation with a fellow passenger. Under this cloud of scandal, Eliza fled to Spain. A year later, she returned to London reinvented as the dancer Maria Dolores de Porris y Montez.

Curiously, at Lola's London "debut," the press heralded her as "purely a Spanish dancer," though interviewers admitted that her accent was hard to place. Her risqué dance was barely in the bounds of decency. They reasoned this was to be expected of a woman of Latin temperament. She was "piquant and provocative"—apparently not yet the cheroot-smoking dame who brandished a dagger or whip. But during Lola's bows, disaster struck. She was recognized as the adulterous wife of Lieutenant James, who was publicly suing for divorce. The crowds jeered and booed. The owner of Her Majesty's Theater closed the show. It was time for the dancer to move on to a new city, pave the highways with fresh scandal, and break a continent of hearts.

Lola kept her "homicidal" temper in check just long enough to charm European aristocrats into securing her theater bookings. Her act was scandalous, for sure, but it was the after-hours carousing that shocked most of all. In Baden-Baden, she threw her leg over a man's shoulder to display her agility, and caused a public outcry at her immorality. In Warsaw, she rudely spurned the advances of the powerful Viceroy. In Dresden, she danced on tabletops at an intimate party for the composer Franz Liszt and destroyed a hotel room. Even as Liszt was paying

the bills for the destruction, he waxed on: "Oh, you must see her!" he wrote of his lover. "She's continually new, continually changing, constantly creative! . . . All other women pale beside her!"

In Munich, Lola reached the height of her scandalous career, as the official mistress of King Ludwig I. Under her influence, Ludwig's cabinet resigned and was replaced with what came to be known as the "Lolaministerium." She set policy and hired staff. She slept with young soldiers (dubbed Lolianers) and clobbered those who offended her. His advisors tattled, but Ludwig wouldn't hear of censuring his fiery royal "muse." Munich rioted, and Lola was spirited out of town. Ludwig was forced to abdicate.

Lola lived on to elude bigamy charges after marrying her second husband without divorcing her first. She challenged an editor to a duel by poison pills. She toured the world and settled down briefly in California, shedding more husbands and lovers than would be wise to list. She wrote a book on beauty and became a popular feminist lecturer. Her advice to women? "Develop the quills of a porcupine," shrug off the servile role, develop the mind, and take up the erotic arts—all the words of a true Competitor. She left us with the expression, "Whatever Lola wants, Lola gets."

Lola's Lesson

When Lola hit town, Ludwig's advisors counseled their king to steer clear—citing the dancer's egregious behavior in European capitals. In Berlin, they told him, she had broken a champagne glass over the head of a soldier who had bothered her with his attentions in a restaurant—and then subsequently spent fourteen days in jail for a whipping incident. Warsaw was still reeling from her "immodest gestures" toward the audience. But the report only piqued good Ludwig's curiosity. On the up side, "the box office would not suffer," they admitted, "because the reputation she has acquired would draw the curious into the theater." The King demanded to see Lola immediately. By nightfall, he was "completely enthralled" with her "fire" and "spirit."

Who was Paris Hilton before the sex tapes? Little more than a spoiled heiress with a sometime modeling career. But after baring all on the Internet, Paris emerged as America's most wanted Sex Kitten, with the exception maybe of Britney. "That's hot" was all Hilton had to say to be booked on a talk show. And when it comes to scandal, we won't soon forget the Rubenesque charms of Monica Lewinsky. Whether she likes it or not, Monica will be dining out for the rest of her life on the affair that brought down an American presidency. It's like the sociologists say: If she's clever, a woman can parlay her sins into celebrity. Scandal only enhances a Siren's cachet. The bigger the brouhaha, the more unforgettable she gets.

CREATE THE APPEARANCE OF SCANDAL

Reluctant to engage in a full-fledged scandal? Just the appearance can create the amount of speculation that is requisite. Take a tip from the White House secretary rumored to be sleeping with JFK—who did his laps and his mistresses in the White House pool. At lunch hour, the secretary drenched her hair every day in the ladies room and then said nothing when she was pelted with inquiring looks.

If history has taught us anything, it's that there's no scandal more captivating than sleeping with a married politician—provided, of course, the indiscretion is leaked to the press. Here, the smart Siren may have to be her own publicist. But maybe a political scandal is a little ambitious and noisy for you. The aspiring Siren need not scale mountain tops; she can build a bad-girl reputation in small ways. Some years ago, I was delighted to find my popularity soar at a wedding when, a little tipsy, I skinny-dipped and wore a tablecloth as a sarong while I dried off.

Dare to do whatever flies in the face of authority—but like Lola, you must do it with a sense of entitlement. Hold your head high. Always pay careful attention to your hair and make-up, particularly if you're headed into court. A trip to rehab or a night in jail may be all you need. Sleep with your boss, or at least let it get around that you did. A cautionary note on blackmail, insider trading, and tax evasion: sensationally scandalous, yes, but these crimes backfire in the end. A Siren doing time has limited access to wardrobe and few men on whom to practice her art.

accentuate the exotic

Josephine Baker

(née Josephine Freda McDonald)

1906–1975

Goddess/Competitor Siren

"Is she horrible? Is she ravishing? Is she black? Is she white?" asked a critic at the opening of *La Revue Nègre* in the fall of 1925. This exotic creature arrived on stage clinging like a vine to another dancer, long legs scissoring skyward in a split. She was shockingly naked, except for a few hot pink feathers tied at her ankles and waist. Slowly cart-wheeling onto the stage, she stood like "an ebony statue"—feral, erotic, and extravagant. A scream of salutation spread through the audience as she raised her arms and quivered in a silent declaration of love, alien, yet recognizable. What happened next hardly mattered anymore. Word of the *Dance au Sauvage* shot through the cafés on the Champs-Elysées, and a Siren legend was born.

"Josephine Baker arrived exactly at the moment we needed her," said an onlooker. She was tonic to a weary, post-war Europe hungry for something new and vital to quicken their blood. Riding the craze for American jazz, Josephine whipped up a concoction of the Charleston, shimmy, and tribal dance that was uniquely her own. It was "eroticism finding a style"—or, as she put it, music expressing its true voice through her. Then there was the unfettered body, whose unusual beauty bewitched and confused. Was she part snake, giraffe, panther, or hummingbird? "She is the Nefertiti of now," said Picasso, settling it once and for all. To this day, France has had only two Josephines. Now, remind me, who was the other one?

How many Goddesses begin life with a Cinderella story? Skinny, homely, neglected, Josephine Freda McDonald came out of the slums of St. Louis with a burning ambition to be seen. She left school at thirteen, married twice as a teen,

102 *simply irresistible*

picking up Baker as her surname. She wriggled her way into a black traveling revue called *Shuffle Along*. Josephine broke rank to do a send-up of the chorus line, introducing her comic eye-rolling and tail spin. The producers were poised to fire her—until the audience begged for more. The legendary skirt of bananas? That came while "La Baker" stormed Paris from the stage of the Folies Bergère.

"A violinist had a violin, a painter his palette. All I had was myself. I was the instrument that I must care for."

—*Josephine Baker*

In Paris, Josephine was an *exotique*, and she was canny enough to play it to the hilt. If she wasn't pictured in designer gowns doing "household chores," she was stark naked under a voluptuous chinchilla—"her breasts handling the fur like silk." Or she promenaded through the streets of Paris in a fanciful cart drawn by an ostrich or with a pet tiger at the end of a leash. There were the green finger-nails, the servants she dressed as sailors, and the menagerie of animals she brought everywhere—among them, a pet pig, a dog that barked *J'ai Deux Amours*, and a monkey that perched on the bathtub rim while she bathed. The icing was *Les Milandes*, the vast château she called home and turned into a kind of Disneyland for the world.

Josephine was "known as much for her legend" as she was for her stage presence. Her "irrational magic" cast a spell even over jaded sophisticates. The artists Picasso, Man Ray, and Jean Cocteau "trailed her about Paris like lovesick puppies." Writer Langston Hughes collected her pictures and press clippings. Hemingway claimed she was "the most beautiful woman there is, there ever was, or ever will be." She promised all the freedom of a wild, new age. The line between performer and citizen was blurred.

Josephine fielded some 1,500 marriage proposals—most, of course, from men she never met. One admirer even offed himself in the street in front of her. During her life, she wed at least five times (though the ceremonies weren't always quite legal)—most notably, to her handler "Pepito," the "no-count Count" who successfully merchandized her image into collectibles. Mercurial, extravagant, averse to the run-of-the-mill, Josephine used all her Goddess wiles to seduce. Until she'd "conquered" a man—or a woman—in the bedroom, something was seriously amiss. She had the sexual rapaciousness of a Competitor Siren.

"I have finished with the exotic," said Josephine, determined to play the bourgeois wife to a new French husband. Her DNA simply wouldn't allow it. She was decorated as a spy in North Africa for the Allies during World War II, where she briefly joined a harem. She returned to the U.S. to star in the Ziegfeld Follies, passing herself off as more French than the French. She adopted a "Rainbow Tribe" of twelve children from all over the world, and plunged herself into spectacular bankruptcy, over and over again. She died just days after a Paris comeback, at which she was greeted like a returning queen.

Josephine's Lesson

"Beautiful? It's all a question of luck. I was born with good legs. As for the rest . . . beautiful, no. Amusing, yes." Josephine shuffled the hand she'd been dealt and found the cards that made her undeniably special. A flair for comedy carried her far. She could perform "the most amazing series of moves with her body" while keeping her eyes crossed. Paris, on the other hand, appreciated something deeper. "I improvised, crazed by the music," said Josephine, "even my teeth and eyes burned with fever. Each time I leaped I seemed to touch the sky and when I regained earth it seemed to be mine alone."

Take away the false eyelashes, the gowns, the headdress made to look like the Eiffel Tower. Outlaw the bananas and the erotic undulations that "gave Paris a hard on." Send the menagerie of animals back to the zoo, and trade Paris for the town where it all began—St. Louis, Missouri. What you've got is Freda McDonald unvarnished—a girl with an oversized ambition to win over the world. "I don't have talent," said Josephine, whose singing voice sounded "like a cracked bell with a padded clapper," at best. She had something better: she was a charismatic original.

Those with charisma offer something off-center, a little out of the norm. That *je ne sais quoi* can come from deep within. At times, it's deliberately layered on. Mata Hari became an exotic by changing her name and dancing the dance of Indonesia. It can take form from a look, a style, an entirely new way of thinking. It can come out of the sheer force of a desire to stand out, along with the conviction that you're pieced together from different cloth. For Josephine, it was her unfailing instinct for what made her a peacock—and then basking in a climate made for exotic birds. Her "magnificent body, a new model to the French," said a critic, "proved for the first time that black was beautiful."

Remember Cher before the plastic surgery? Her Roman nose became a must-have item for those who wanted to intrigue. Then, of course, there were the outrageous costumes she had constructed on some far more glamorous planet and shipped to Hollywood. For some, a new locale can make all the difference; it certainly helped catapult Josephine. Even if they don't have a clue what you're saying, your accent alone has exotic appeal. What makes you different? Maybe you were raised by gypsies, moved here from Malta, or are curiously marked by fate in some way.

Toss out those how-to books and articles that tell a woman what she should be (except, of course, this one). Instead of downplaying your differences, incorporate them into what makes you more interesting. Even an imperfection can mark you as the unusual seductress you are, as long as you play it with confidence. A woman I know parlayed the beet-red birthmark on her cheekbone into her signature look—and she did it with such élan, it would make you want one of your own. It only takes a little exotica, baby, for the whole thing to grow.

Maybe you've traveled and slept with kings, or have an unusual talent, an off-beat style, or a cock-eyed way of seeing the world. Could be you're an underworld spy or a tightrope walker at the circus. Whatever it is, work it, baby—unless what separates you from the pack is little more than an aggravated case of OCD. In that case, consider this: in Spain or Tahiti, you could be celebrated as the next new thing. Let me be the first to wish you bon voyage! Pack some bananas in case you need some clothes.

ARE YOU UNFORGETTABLE?

Are you a legend—or do you suffer merely from being a legend in your own mind? The more questions to which you answer "yes," the more memorable you are. If you say "no" to all, it may be time to return to the drawing board.

✦ Do men tend to remember you after the first time you've been introduced?

✦ Do others have a favorite story or stories about you they like to tell?

✦ Have you ever created a scandal of any kind, either on purpose or inadvertently?

✦ If so, did you enjoy it?

✦ Are you unafraid of doing or saying things that may not be entirely correct?

✦ Do you have a distinctive scent that others find delicious?

✦ Do you seek settings and situations where you are more likely to stand out than blend in?

✦ Are you unconcerned about what others may think of you?

✦ Are you considered eccentric or "one of a kind"?

✦ Do you like to make an entrance?

✦ Does the way you dress make you stand out in some way?

✦ Do you have a talent for something, large or small, for which you are recognized?

Put Your Best
Foot Forward

Sirens are not necessarily beautiful, it's true. The pages of *Simply Irresistible*, in fact, are filled with women whose seductive power has little to do with conventional prettiness. Yet, it's in a Siren's nature to take stock of her physical charms. It's part instinct, part pride, and it contributes to her unassailable confidence. Siren or not, aren't we all in the business of selling ourselves?

A Siren makes the most of her assets. That's not to say you'll never catch her lounging around in a paint-stained t-shirt with her hair unwashed. In truth, there are times and places when that kind of dishevelment is appropriate. But when it counts, the seductress uses all her available resources. What to do with her hair and clothes? These are among the strategic decisions—and pleasures—of womanhood. But there are more ways to put your best foot forward than you might first think. Consider the total effect of your presence.

Many seductresses are stylish, but Jackie Kennedy made style her philosophy. What's more, she overcame what she saw as a long list of physical flaws and looked supremely fashionable. Nicole Kidman's tresses? On a good hair day, what man wouldn't want to get lost in them? Margaretha Zelle ramped up her Siren powers as Mata Hari; she has a valuable lesson to teach aspiring seductresses about choosing a handle that works. The Divine Sarah Bernhardt, the first international superstar, seduced with the music in her voice. In this chapter, we'll meet the women who are and were the "marketing experts" of the Siren world.

let down your hair

Nicole Kidman

1967–

Goddess Siren

It is the spring of 1861, and the men of Cold Mountain are preparing to fight against the North in the Civil War. But the searching glances and shy words between W.P. Inman and Ada Monroe tell another story: Love with a capital L. Or maybe it's sex dressed up in corsets and crinolines. As shots are fired at Fort Sumter, Inman is called to war. He kisses Ada passionately and she promises to wait. Three years later, he deserts ranks and flees home on foot to Ada. Hey, these two kids are barely acquainted. Yet we know their love is real because of Ada's hair—locks so luscious they're worth all the risks Inman takes to get home.

If you muted the sound from *Cold Mountain*, starring Nicole Kidman and Jude Law, the story could be told by the ups and downs of Ada's hair. Early on , her locks are wound tight, like our belle. When war breaks out, a bird could mistake her tangles for a nesting place. As Inman draws closer to home, Ada's full, golden hair unfurls to her waist, and wild strands signal her willing sexuality. She's Rapunzel, save the turret, reeling in her prince. As the two collide, Ada's tendrils wrap around their bodies in a love scene straight out of a fairy tale.

If you're going to make a film with a subplot for hair, you would do well to cast Nicole as the head from which it grows. Hers is one of the most watched heads of hair, or so says an online survey of men. Her Siren status is embellished—even confirmed—by that hair. And knowing its seductive power, Kidman uses it judiciously. In her youth, she wore her tumbling mane wild and free. It said, "cast me, I'll show you unexpected sexuality." As her reputation grew, the guarded Goddess came out in tight chignons and ponytails. Today, in love, Kidman lets it fall

straight to her shoulders, a sleek version of her early Siren self.

Born into Australia's liberal version of the Cleaver family, Kidman showed a Goddess's proclivity for being the oddball. "I had a huge desire to be someone else," she said. She was teased for her height, her ghostly skin, and that unruly hair. On a modeling job, a hairdresser shaped her mane into ringlets and the "pre-Raphaelite angel" was born. She morphed into Venus on a half shell. "Nic found her essence just simply through allowing her hair to be what it is naturally," said a friend.

While Kidman casts herself as the Aussie next door, the image is a little spun. She uses words like "destiny" when discussing the roles for which she's actually fought like a gladiator. During her ten-year union to actor Tom Cruise, Kidman looked all but made of marble. Through an intercepted cell phone exchange, we learned that Cruise met her Goddess-like demands for flowers, drawn baths, and love notes. The marriage was perfect—until the shocker divorce. We'll never know what exactly went down. She's since recast herself as country singer Keith Urban's sainted wife.

Kidman rules Hollywood with her air of mystery, which persists even as she indulges a public demand for frank talk. We watch that hair for some indication of what's going on. For roles, it's been short, black, strawberry, curly, and straight, but men love her most as a pre-Raphaelite—*Days of Thunder*, *Malice*, *Far and Away*, or *Moulin Rouge*'s tubercular Satine come to mind. Only in those ads for Chanel No. 5—the Siren's scent—is the voltage truly turned up. Without those locks, would she be the Goddess she is today?

Nicole's Lesson

Did Eve tempt Adam with a cute bob? Did Helen of Troy launch ships with a buzz cut? Can you think of a song that praises short hair over long? I think not. It's "Gimme a head with hair, long beautiful hair/Shining, gleaming, streaming, flaxen, waxen/Give me down to there, hair!" If you need further proof, look to actress Keri Russell, who played television's angelic Felicity. She cut her hair, and the ratings plummeted. Shorn of their manes, Gwyneth Paltrow, Jennifer Aniston, and Sarah Jessica Parker all have cautionary tales.

"All I know is I've never gotten a complaint from a man about long hair," said actress Jane Seymour, a Siren herself. Well, you won't. No woman alive will dispute this preference. But what's it all about, anyway? Early Christians had a notion that a dame's locks were part of her genitalia—capable of drawing semen like an amorous Hoover. The theory echoes what men and women instinctively know: great hair is equal to powerful sex appeal. Why else would women be forced to cover it up in much of the world? Even men equate their baldness with a lack of virility.

A woman with fabulous long locks has an electric effect. Kidman gets just how much clout comes from her hair, and doesn't appear in public without having calculated which strand falls where. Up in a twist, a loose pin or two could bring it tumbling down, the classic image of the prim librarian with a sensual soul. Long hair signals youth, but what if, like Kidman, you've crept, albeit beautifully, into your forties? "The age factor is totally bogus," says *Vogue*. In fact, "short hair cut like a helmet can make a young woman look old." Demi Moore, Jane Seymour, and Rene Russo all know: long hair deepens your sex appeal.

INDULGE THE SCHOOLYARD FANTASY

Eva Perón wore them when she kicked back with Juan. Nicole sports them when she wants to be coy. "Guys adore pigtails," says my Siren friend Samantha. Colette promoted pigtails in her salacious novel *Claudine at School*, and Parisian brothels took the cue. Pull your hair into braids or pigtails occasionally. If you dare, pair it with a girlish kilt. As Samantha says, "it's the whole sex and the schoolgirl fantasy come true."

At odds about what to do with your hair? Grow it. Do whatever you must to make it luscious and thick. A Siren never, ever gets practical when it comes to doing her hair. Don't make the mistake of cutting it because it's newly chic, a bother, or too thin. According to experts, anything above the jaw line is taking a risk—unless you're one of those very rare birds who looks good with it snipped. In the wise words of Martin Luther, "The hair is the richest ornament of women." Grow it, fluff it, and style it to your heart's content. Hair pieces? They're a godsend.

strive to be chic

Jacqueline Lee Bouvier Kennedy Onassis

1929–1994

Goddess/Companion Siren

"I want to be the best-dressed woman in the world, without appearing to be the best-dressed woman in the world," said Jacqueline Kennedy. In the weeks before the newly minted First Lady traveled abroad in 1961, she and fashion designer Oleg Cassini worked feverishly putting together her wardrobe. "You have an opportunity here," said Cassini, pausing, "for an American Versailles"—to present the U.S. Presidency as in league with old-world royalty. But there was considerable risk of going overboard. What if she looked like a fashion-crazed Marie Antoinette and they demanded her head? "So winning was she," in her red Cardin suit, her Cassini silk-and-wool dress, in the pink chiffon evening gown adorned with sequins, that heads of state became unglued. "I am the man who accompanied Jacqueline Kennedy to Paris," the President joked. By the end of 1961, Jackie was featured as Woman of the Year by magazines around the world.

"Here was a woman, at least expressed by clothes, who had a crystal-clear vision of who she was and how she wanted to be portrayed," wrote a journalist in hindsight. She was no Eleanor, no Mamie Eisenhower. She wanted to follow in the footsteps of the nineteenth-century Siren Madame de Récamier (of reclining fame), whose great style and salon profoundly influenced France's court life. "I don't want to go down into coal mines or be a symbol of elegance," said Jackie. "I will never be a committee woman or a club woman, because I'm not a joiner." Blending old-world values with new, she aimed to present Americans as the world's first modern sophisticates. They say it was the closest fashion ever got to politics.

If there was ever such a thing as an American aristocracy, Jacqueline Lee Bouvier was born in the thick of it. Despite that, Janet and Jack Bouvier—divorced early on—would send their daughter into the world with shaky confidence. But this is where Goddess seeds are often sown. As a teenager, Jackie's seductive power came from her silence, as later her enduring stardom would. Her elegance made her Debutante of the Year. While she studied at Vassar, young men were constantly trying every kind of trick to make her go out with them. The budding Goddess stayed aloof—dreamy, bookish, and maddeningly off on her own. After a year in France, Jackie returned determined to lead a life of consequence. She broke an engagement that would have led to life on Park Avenue, sipping cocktails nightly before dinner at eight.

Jackie was twenty-four years old to Jack Kennedy's thirty-seven when they met. She took photographs for a Washington newspaper. He was preparing for a Senate bid and honing his reputation as a womanizer. Sophisticated, smart, and seemingly self-possessed, Jackie was the kind of challenge that Jack couldn't resist—but he wasn't always as attentive as he might have been. When she felt ignored, Jackie did what Goddesses do best. She didn't return his calls or disappeared for the weekend without a word. When Jack proposed marriage, she made him wait weeks for the answer while she toured the Continent. (Don't you just love her self-control?) She knew he would never be faithful but was lured by visions of his promised life, what was later called Camelot.

GO VINTAGE

Vintage clothing enhances the Goddess Siren's distancing effect. A Victorian blouse or Fifties-style frock sends you back in time, forcing him to struggle that much harder to grasp the eternally mysterious you.

"She had a keen sense of her place in history," wrote journalist Marie Brenner in *Great Dames*. Jackie wasn't aiming to change the lot of women but to wield powerful influence as the first helpmate and Companion. She worked on Jack's speeches and edited his book. He relied on her instinct for character. She redecorated the White House and invited the scions of high culture to share their meals. Jackie reigned as the American Queen in matters of taste, which ran in her bloodstream. When they met, Pope John XXIII threw open his arms and cried "Jack-eee!" The Soviet Union's Khrushchev famously brushed past JFK to get to the First Lady. When he saw the returns, Jackie's father-in-law, Joe, footed the bill for her wardrobe. Hoping to attain the Jackie allure, women donned A-line shifts, pillbox hats, and pastel suits. Jackie not only changed the way the world saw us, but how we viewed ourselves.

As the widow of JFK, Jackie continued to be among the world's most watched celebrities—like Princess Diana, she was the obsession of paparazzi everywhere. She married Aristotle Onassis, the boorish shipping tycoon, and then divorced. She became a New York book editor, and made any event she attended fashionable. A half century later, her legend lives on. She is forever the First Lady we will remember for her clothes.

Jackie's Lesson

"As to physical appearance, I am tall, five-foot-seven, with brown hair, a square face and eyes so unfortunately far apart that it takes three weeks to have a pair of glasses made with a bridge wide enough to fit over my nose," Jackie wrote in an application for *Vogue*'s Prix de Paris while she was at Vassar. "I do not have a sensational figure but I can look slim if I pick the right clothes." Hey, Jackie had issues just like the rest of us. True, she had a knack for putting on a classic dress or pair of pants, and making it chic with the right belt. That unerring sense of style was key to her appeal. But don't kid yourself, Jackie thought long and hard about what worked.

Before Jackie, women wore gathered skirts, cinched waists, and puffed sleeves. She conformed to no fashion standard and ushered in a streamlined silhouette. "We look at her and think, 'How simple!'" said Givenchy. "But . . . she was very conscious of her style, her body, her face." She "instinctively knew what...flattered her," wrote another fashionista, "and what decidedly didn't." She stuck to solid colors, classic lines, and sporty clothes. She wore empire-waisted gowns to lengthen her legs and boat-neck tops to draw eyes to her elegant collarbone. By looking singularly fabulous, she "broke the mold of what had come to characterize the ideally desirable American woman." The fantasy buxom blonde of the 1950s was joined by the sporty, dark sophisticate.

APPLY PAINT WITH CARE

Cleopatra wrote a treatise on cosmetics. Lola Montez published her beauty tips. What courtesan Cora Pearl had in the way of beauty was painted on. If a girl could use a boost from her powder puff, she should at least learn how to put on her make-up so it looks great. A Siren's true power comes from within—but she hates a shiny nose.

What is style? "For some, it's a kind of consistent rightness about clothes that distinguishes the would-be chic from the real elite," says *The Power of Style*. But what it's *not* is a closet full of designer labels bought for the names alone. I know a woman of substance who would spend top dollar on a burlap bag tied with a string if the tag said Chanel; nobody can ever quite make out what she's got on. Even as a student, Jackie wasn't a slave to trends. She stuck to a cloth coat when minks were all the rage. "I flatter myself at times of being able to walk out of the house looking like the poor man's Paris copy," young Jackie wrote in all modesty. To be chic, know what makes you look best and wear it like you're on the runway.

As First Lady, Jackie deliberately chose to mesmerize the world with her brand of chic. Or as she said: "I want to make Jack look like *he* is the French President." But maybe you're casting your spell a little closer to home—and regal is not quite the look you're going for; which reminds me of my dear departed Aunt Esther, rest her fashionable soul. Unadorned, Esther looked like a wide-eyed gnome, and yet she put her clothes together splendidly. "She's chic," my mother claimed. I only saw that she managed to look pretty, even though I couldn't figure out how she'd pulled it all together. Esther could have accessorized that Chanel burlap sack, and come out with something flatteringly original. Always immaculately groomed, she spent every penny of her hard-earned cash on the best of what made her look incredible. Fuchsia, silk, sling-back shoes. Let's just say Esther had a keen sense of her assets and dressed to kill.

Find clothes that flatter your womanly figure, even if it takes mining fashion ideas from another decade. Try not to look like you're afflicted with fashion jet lag: i.e., forget football-player-sized padded shoulders, unless you're headed to a costume party as *Dynasty*'s Krystle Carrington. Wear the hues that bring out the flush in your cheeks and the twinkle in your eyes, and, of course, black flatters everyone. Go for the striking detail, and put the parts together in a way that's wholly original. Don't be ashamed to seek outside help. (Jackie did.) Don't follow trends unless they work. Stick to the well-made classics if you're unsure.

If it fits like an overcoat, get yourself to the best tailor in town. Whatever you've got on your back, it should look like it's custom made with you in mind. Remember that fashion is a language. Figure out what you'd like to say; don't speak in incomplete sentences or dangle your modifiers. What you wear should make you feel beautiful. Style has drawing power; your Siren chic can be an irresistible lure.

YOU MAY ALSO BE INTERESTED TO KNOW THAT JACKIE...

✦ Always maintained flawless posture (which she learned as an equestrienne).

✦ Dieted as soon as she was even two pounds over her ideal weight.

✦ Sprinkled cologne on her brush and gave her hair fifty strokes every night.

✦ "Glistened" her eyelashes with a pinch of skin cream.

✦ Applied powder to her lips before and after lipstick ("should stay on . . . through corn on the cob").

find your wooing voice

Sarah Bernhardt

1844–1923

Companion/Goddess Siren

When she finally finagled a meeting with master director Félix Duquesnel in 1866, actress Sarah Bernhardt had been out of work for nearly two years. She prepared as she might for a critical stage entrance. She arrived exotically costumed in a *crepe de chine* tunic of Chinese cut and a wide straw hat with bells that jingled prettily with every move. "Before my eyes appeared one of the most ideal charmers you could ever dream of," reported the dazzled Duquesnel. "She was more than pretty, much more dangerous than that! . . . Pure as crystal, [her voice] went straight to my heart. . . . I was conquered body and soul." Duquesnel snapped up Sarah for his bed and for the Odéon Theater, where she became a *tour de force*.

Before television, before radio, before *People* magazine had been invented, Sarah Bernhardt was the first international superstar—an icon on par with the Arc de Triomphe. Her every throat-clearing was reported in the press. Bernhardt was tiny (just over five feet) and "skeletally" thin. Her frizzy mop of reddish hair brought to mind Raggedy Ann. Even her motto—*quand même*, or, even so—makes one wonder: what was it that made her so irresistible? Time and again, her magnetic appeal was chalked up to her smoldering eyes, her graceful gestures, but most of all to her wooing voice. "I believed at once everything she said," wrote a young Sigmund Freud, bewitched by her performance in *Théodora*. She was called the greatest actress of all time, The Divine Sarah, the Eighth Wonder of the World.

The neglected daughter of a busy Parisian courtesan, young Sarah developed an insatiable need to have the world pay court. She stoked it on the stages of the

Odéon and the Comédie Française, before forming her own international touring company. That she slept in a coffin added a delightfully bizarre spin to her appeal—and gave her the extra ink she craved. Like most actresses of her day, Sarah entertained "sponsors." She learned early on to juggle the *amant de coeurs*—the lovers who had her heart—with those of means. Debt, for Sarah, "was only a springboard to greater extravagance." The entrances and exits of those promiscuous years fed her stagecraft. She conquered Paris and then London with her romantic take on classics like *La Dame aux Camélias (Camille)*. "I could love such a woman myself, love her to madness," wrote D. H. Lawrence, of her death scene. "Her sad, plaintive little murmurs; her terrible panther cries . . . the little sobs that fairly sear one . . . it is too much in one evening." Was this the birth of the modern soap opera?

"My dear colleague, why attack me so violently? Actors ought not to be so hard on one another."

—Sarah Bernhardt's published response to the Bishop of Montreal's attack on her work

Sarah thrived on a "grueling combination" of love and work—each offering suspense, climaxes, and curtain calls. "Come! Come! Come!" she wrote to a lover, and enclosed her drawing of a rumpled four-poster bed. To another, it was, "For me, to love is to love you," even as her lovers overlapped. She had the Companion's knack for delivering the sweet words her admirers longed to hear. She was at her best as sage advisor and champion of their careers. Yet with every advance, she beat the Goddess's hasty retreat, often into an intrigue, a new *amoureuse*. "I am not well, my friend Jean, not well at all. I do not dare to bring this sick little being to see you." After several rounds, poor tortured Jean kicked in a coachman's window in a jealous rage. Still, he begged not to be released from her "pretty pink claws."

Of Sarah, it was said that, "lovemaking was the quickest road to friendship." The inconstant mistress was a loyal and entertaining friend—isn't it always the way with the Companion? Her circle included the Prince of Wales, the writer Victor Hugo, and the artist Gustave Doré, as well as countless actors, directors, playwrights, and assorted financiers. "My heart demands more excitement than anyone can give it," she wrote. There was a flash-in-the-pan marriage to a younger Greek actor, whose appeal barely survived the wedding day. As she aged, Sarah kept her "monstrous vitality" and every piquant note of her wooing voice. At age sixty-six, her twenty-seven-year-old lover declared that Sarah's *"enchantée de faire votre connaissance!"* (charmed to meet you) became "a Beethoven symphony. I understand why she is called 'the woman with the golden voice.'"

In her seventies, the indomitable Sarah performed from her sedan chair after having her right leg amputated because of an injured knee. She moved into the new medium of film, famously playing the Siren Queen Elizabeth I. Bernhardt would go down in history for the "glamour of her personality," to quote Oscar Wilde, and the seductive power of her speaking voice.

Sarah's Lesson

Early in Sarah's career, the Odéon Theater planned to produce a play by the popular writer Victor Hugo, but Napoleon III insisted that they substitute a play by the imperial favorite, Alexandre Dumas. Paris was outraged and gathered at the theater to protest. The rowdy demonstration wore on for an hour before the curtain rose, while the mob continued with their angry "crescendo of ear-shattering catcalls." Sarah strode resolutely down to the footlights. "Do you think you are encouraging justice by holding Alexandre Dumas responsible for Victor Hugo's exile?" she asked. A thoughtful silence fell. "Mlle. Bernhardt appeared in an eccentric costume," reported *L'Opinion Nationale*, "but her warm voice, her astonishing voice, moved the public. Like a little Orpheus, she tamed it."

PRACTICE MAKES PURR-FECT

Want to give your voice that wooing tone? Greatvoice.com advises finding a word that represents seductive for you—like "sultry"—and repeating it out loud three times. Then, call up a corresponding mental image (for me, most nonviolent scenes from the television series *Rome*). Relax your face, give 'em your impish grin, and practice saying, "I'm not that kind of girl," until you definitely are.

In the florid language of the day, Sarah's voice was described as "silvery," "a caress," and "like the sighs the wind draws from an Aeolian harp." Her delivery was "so true in rhythm, so clear in utterance," a critic wrote in *Le Temps*, that "not a single syllable was lost." Her voice had a musical quality. Using it like an instrument, she lulled the listener into her confidence with high and low notes. In her take on the role of Hamlet, "To be or not to be" was a "contemplative murmur," rather than the declamation that was the standard of the day. Her tone projected a startling new emotional expressiveness that moved them to tears.

Think voice isn't as important as, say, the right shade of lipstick? Consider that when silent films became "talkies" back in the late twenties and thirties, stars whose voices didn't hold up on screen lost their careers. In sitcoms and movies today, characters with annoying voices are the foils for the romantic leads. But what exactly is it that makes a woman's voice appealing to men? According to NPR, it's hard to pinpoint, but it may have something to do with breathiness, particularly in the lower octaves. Kathleen Turner's Jessica Rabbit, for instance, gets high marks. Jane Fonda's voice became sexy when she dropped it to play a call girl in the movie *Klute*. But according to a UCLA study of phone sales, there's something more practical at work. It's the "music"—pitch, tone, and inflection—that makes or breaks the deal. It's not so much its quality, in other words, but the personality behind the voice that's key.

READ HIM A BEDTIME STORY

Poetry, pornography, *The Little Engine That Could*—use that beautiful voice of yours to read him a bedtime story with cookies and milk. "I began doing it by accident while I was rehearsing lines for a play," says Holly, a former actress turned currency trader. "I found out that it had erotic potential." Reading to a man has not only a Mother Siren's soothing effect, but it also has potentially interesting powers of suggestion if you choose the right reading material.

If your voice sounds like a cartoon character or a low-flying airplane, do what actors do: work at changing it. If you're not sure, tape yourself. A voice coach can work wonders in a single session. Gorgeous hair, a buff torso, smooth skin, and dazzling teeth are worth the investment; why not a voice that can turn them on? Men claim they can be talked into anything if a woman's voice is sexy enough. It's what gives him his gut feeling about you when you meet for the first time. Your voice is your identity—do you really want it to say you're a snore? Seductive, sweet, or shrill, speech telegraphs more than you know.

A seductress never lets haste, irritation, or boredom creep into her speech—unless, of course, she means to. Like Sarah Bernhardt, she aims to project warm intimacy, to reach out to the listener, and to take him into her confidence. Charm them with your dulcet tones. Seduce them with words. You could be wooing them with a simple "charmed to meet you," if you use the right tone. The voice that's a pleasure is the voice that's heard. Nothing is quite as seductive—forever—as the woman who is easy to listen to.

Skin. Always in . . .

change your name

Mata Hari

(née Margaretha Geertruida Zelle)

1876–1917

Sex Kitten Siren

As the plaintive chords of a lone sitar filled the makeshift temple, a dancer appeared in dramatic silhouette. Slowly, rhythmically, she moved with passionate abandon before a graven image of Siva, a Hindu god with an apparent appetite for female flesh. She discarded her flowing veils, one by one, revealing her long, glistening limbs, quivering loins, and metallic bustier. In a crescendo of religious fervor, she gave herself up to Siva in delirious submission, carrying "the male—and a good proportion of the female—spectators to the limit of decent attention." For the invited audience, the name Mata Hari added another glittering layer of exotic mystery to the spectacle. When the house lights came up, she was Lady MacLeod, a highborn divorcée of Indonesian descent.

Like any aspiring Siren, Grete MacLeod knew the power of spin. And as a Belle Epoque courtesan, she saw the need to distinguish herself in a market glut of beautiful girls. Drawing on years spent living in the Dutch West Indies, she recreated herself as an exotic dancer from a Hindu temple. She virtually invented striptease, and made it semi-respectable with a spiritual veneer. Her success was her "brazen novelty." Newspapers reported on her conquests, "delighting in mocking each new victim of her charms" as he was discarded for a successful rival. Mata Hari's genius was the name, which, roughly translated from Indonesian means "light of day."

Margaretha Geertruida Zelle was born in Leeuwarden, Holland, the daughter of a hatter with social pretensions. Looking for high adventure at eighteen, Grete answered a personals ad in an Amsterdam newspaper (she'd be cruising the Internet today, no doubt): "Captain in the Army of the Indies, on leave in Holland seeks wife with a character to his taste." She sailed off to the Dutch West Indies as the young bride of Captain Rudolf MacLeod. Alas, theirs was far from a happy home. His drinking was a prelude to violence and wholesale philandering. At age twenty-seven, the marriage at an end, Grete landed in Paris looking for work as an artist's model.

NEED TO KNOW DEPT.

Mata Hari had many, *many* lovers, none of whom ever managed to see her completely naked. She was ashamed of her breasts, but the reason was a mystery. She claimed—gruesomely—that her husband had bitten off her nipples in a drunken rage, but like much of Mata Hari's back-story, this was generally considered to be untrue. In bed, Mata always wore a heavily padded bustier that she had had specially made.

Every Sex Kitten has a Pygmalion. Grete met hers in the older Baron Henry de Marguérie, second secretary of The Hague's French legation. He picked up her hotel bill and together they shaped her novelty stage act. At five feet nine inches, Grete was unfashionably tall and lanky, but the Kittenish swing of her hips had magical appeal. The unveiling of the great Mata Hari, temple dancer, at a Paris museum became instant hot copy—though, as the writer Colette noted, "she hardly danced at all." In "yonder India," where she'd never been, "two lovers really love," Mata Hari explained, "actually engage in the love embrace on the stage in full view of the audience." Of course, she was having them on.

Mata Hari never practiced "the simpler arts of coquetry so familiar to the chic *Parisienne*," wrote an admirer. There was "something of the primitive savage," and yet something also "refined," about her. Sex was more important to men than women in her view. A woman's power came from using that knowledge aggressively. Her provocative approach, it was said, made it difficult for a man not to be lured. As infallibly as sugar and arsenic charm flies, they swarmed. But her Hindu aim of "living in beauty" really meant she was constantly on the prowl for cheap thrills.

Hers was "not the beauty that bloomed for one man, but for the multitude"—

which included the Crown Prince of Germany, War Minister Adolphe-Pierre Messimy, the composers Giacomo Puccini and Jules Massenet, and Baron Henry de Rothschild. She preferred soldiers, as they gave her the chance to "compare nations," she said, without a hint of irony. Her shtick was lavish seduction—"I conquered him"—and then total submission—"do with me what you wish." The combination intoxicated. At the outbreak of World War I, she fell deeply in love with a young Russian soldier half her age. After she was forced to support him, she entered the spy game.

"This was perhaps the greatest woman spy of the century," said the prosecutor at Mata Hari's trial for espionage. "The evil [she] has done is unbelievable." Mata Hari was, in fact, recruited to spy for the French, who mistakenly thought she was turning over information to the Germans. She was actually more of a bumbler caught up in the frenzy of war; she was convicted on flimsy evidence. The great Mata Hari died dressed to the nines, blowing kisses to her firing squad.

Mata Hari's Lesson

If Renaissance Italy was known for painters and sculptors, then turn-of-the-century Paris goes down as the era of the courtesan, who made love an art and sex a respectable profession. But the names of the greats—Harriet Wilson, Alice Ozy, or even Blanche de Païva—have all but faded into oblivion. Grete MacLeod knew that what becomes a legend most is an unforgettable handle. The name Mata Hari still means seductress, even to those who know nothing of Grete MacLeod today.

When Grete launched her act at Paris's Musée Guimet, the director insisted that she use a stage name. She proposed Mata Hari, the one she had used in Indonesia while performing "native dance" at the officers' club. The name sounded deeply exotic but was easy to remember and pronounceable. In no time, men developed a Pavlovian response: the name "Mata Hari" alone was an instant turn on. Officers salivated on hearing that Mata Hari was in the room.

Norma Jean Baker, Beryl Clutterbuck, and Bessie Wallis Warfield became Marilyn Monroe, Beryl Markham, and Wallis, Duchess of Windsor. Eliza Gilbert was Lola Montez, and Greta Lovisa Gustafson, the mysterious Garbo. Pamela Digby continued to list the surname Churchill, even after she had divorced Winston's son and taken other husbands. Why? Because it made her feel good. (*And*, of course, because she was a terrible snob.) If your name makes you feel like a Cinderella before the ball, don't hesitate. Change it to something more befitting your Siren self. It makes as much of an impression as the clothes you wear, and it's far less expensive than staying fashionable. Choose the right name, and it will boost your image tenfold.

Did we discuss my college classmate Brett Ashley? If you recognize her name, you're not alone. It's from *The Sun Also Rises*, Ernest Hemingway's classic novel we all read in school. As a freshman, the former Natalie Fink saw her opportunity to start over again. Like Hemingway's heroine, Natalie had a way with men, but "Brett" made her feel that she was entitled to have it. Sometimes, all you need to change is a vowel or syllable. A plain Jane I know became Janu; my friend Linda is now the Lana she long dreamt she was. Both report their names have made a difference in how they feel about themselves and, consequently, in the way others respond.

MAKE IT LEGAL

You can pick a new name and consistently use it, or make it forever yours through the court system. But forget "Carmen Electra" if your intent is to cash in on the actress's celebrity. Know that punctuation, numbers, and naughty words are also out, unless, apparently, you're Prince. The paperwork is different from state to state, but if you want to make it legal, the place to begin is your county courthouse. Go to soyouwanna.com to find out how.

Feeling a little awkward about answering to Tallulah? This is what towns like Las Vegas are for. Take a test run. Spin a little roulette, baby, and toss back a cocktail while wearing the name of your choice. Do Cancun next spring as Venus de Milo. If the name settles effortlessly, it might be the one destined for you. Back home, there's no need to insist. Introduce yourself to strangers with your new handle, and eventually others will go along. If a simple "Kate" makes you feel sexy, turn it on. Or work it in reverse. In time, "Hortense" may take after the Siren in you.

ARE YOU PUTTING YOUR BEST FOOT FORWARD?

Are you stuck in a rut? Or are you mixing it up—constantly looking for bold, new ways to express the seductress in you? The more questions to which you can answer "yes," the better. Say "no" more often than not, and it may be time for a makeover.

+ Do you dress to make an impression?

+ Can you easily list the colors and styles that most flatter you?

+ Do you consider your hair to be one of your "essential ornaments"?

+ Do you spend more time styling your hair than you do on showering?

+ Are you conscious of using your voice to achieve the best results when you make a demand or request?

+ Do you feel that time spent on personal presentation is time well spent?

+ Do you have style mentors—women whose overall presentation you feel is worth emulating?

+ Does your name reflect your personality?

+ Are you willing to try new things? (Or do you feel you've found your permanent style niche?)

+ Do you believe that, in spite of your flaws, you are an attractive-looking person?

+ Do you feel that on some level, everyone is in the business of selling themselves?

Transport Them

Some Sirens have a knack for taking a man out of himself. It's the law of the universe: when she makes him feel good, she becomes irresistible. She may make him laugh just at the moment when he needs it most, or have him feeling like a CEO, even as he's pulling in the salary of a mailroom clerk. Other Sirens spur his soul into a creativity he never knew possible. The Siren's gift lies in finding his pleasure points and working them. She knows exactly what to say and do.

You won't be surprised to learn that the seductress who transports most reliably is a Companion or Mother Siren—sometimes, she's a Sex Kitten. For her, the act of giving him pleasure is often reward in itself. It's part of her essential nature. Yet, a Goddess or Competitor Siren can deliver as transcendent an experience as her sisters when she chooses to. Whatever her archetype, a Siren is the most wily and flexible of females.

Would a look at seductresses who transport be complete without the infamous Pamela Harriman? In five minutes or less, she could make a man feel as if he were the axis on which the world spins. Celebrity chef Nigella Lawson mixes the joy of sex with the joy of cooking, and no one's complained so far. Actress Carole Lombard made 'em laugh, and the sixteenth-century courtesan Veronica Franco got paid for her transcendent conversation. Were it not for the muse in Alma Mahler, we have to ask: would we have some of our greatest works of art today?

make him the center of the universe

Pamela Digby Churchill Hayward Harriman

1920–1997

Mother/Companion Siren

In the "awful . . . dark" summer of 1971, the Broadway producer Leland Hayward died, leaving his widow with many debts. At fifty-one, Pamela Digby Churchill Hayward might have wondered if she was quite as fetching as she once had been. An unexpected invitation arrived from the publisher Katharine Graham: Would Pam come to her "little dinner" for sixty guests? Here, perhaps, was a silver lining. At the dinner, Pam spotted Averell Harriman, a former lover, and skillfully switched her place card—seating herself back-to-back from him at adjacent tables so the move wasn't too obvious. During dinner, she swung around and focused her laser-steady attention on the wealthy statesman, who at seventy-nine, was nearly deaf. "She looked him straight in the eye and took care to enunciate clearly and avoided rolling her r's in the Churchillian cadence" she usually affected, wrote a biographer, and she hung, breathless, on his every word. Within a month, Pam had added "Harriman" to her long list of surnames.

Pamela Harriman was arguably the very last of the great courtesans—that is, a woman who lived "independently" for a time by her sexual wits. Her three husbands were all strategically picked. "What is your secret?" Barbra Streisand dared to ask on meeting the notorious Pam, who was neither beautiful, especially smart, witty, nor even original. Even her champions admitted the raw material was thin. But she had the undeniable "ability to make a man feel supreme." Men basked in the attention. She put her lovers at the center of the universe, adapting herself like a chameleon to their every whim.

The daughter of the eleventh Baron Digby, Pamela grew up at Minterne Magna, a fifty-room ancestral mansion in Dorset, England—though for all the apparent luxury, the Digbys were cash poor. She was descended from the scandalous Lady Jane Digby, who, in the nineteenth century, was censured by the British Parliament for adultery. Jane lived out the end of her exotic life in Arabia, lovingly washing the feet of a Bedouin prince. Whereas Pam's parents shoved this bit of Digby history under the rug, Pam used it as a starting point. She "decided early on that she was going to turn herself into a very glamorous person," said her sister.

At age nineteen, Pam married Randolph Churchill, a drunk and a gambler, on the strength of three dates. His appeal was his wartime absence and the Churchill name. Winston took an instant shine to his red-haired daughter-in-law, and she zeroed in. On call during the London blitz, she playing bezique through the night with the insomniac Prime Minister (her "Papa") and became his trusty sounding board. Young Pam Churchill rode high in London as a wartime hostess to generals and diplomats. Always the "fixer," Mother Pam was "the girl you called if you wanted anything—a flat, theater tickets, cars, restaurants," said a friend. Winston used her to probe the intentions of important visiting Americans. She saw glamorous opportunity in older, powerful, married men she romanced— notably, the journalist Edward R. Murrow and Averell Harriman. While she wasn't quite beautiful, Pam had twinkling eyes, masses of hair, alabaster skin, and a good figure; but more importantly, she made men feel good.

"I would rather have bad things written about me than be forgotten."

—Pamela Harriman

"She was extraordinary in the way she took care of her men," said paramour Bill Paley, CBS Chairman. Before a man realized his throat was parched, she put a glass in his hand; his weary head always hit the pillow she had waiting for him. Post-war, Pamela divorced Randolph and moved to Paris. Over the next decade, her amorous "sponsors" included Gianni Agnelli, Aly Khan, Elie de Rothschild, and Stavros Niarchos.

By the early sixties, Pam was casting her net into American waters. She moved in while "wives were off duty"—as always. "Are you happy in your marriage?" she asked the ravishing Slim Keith, wife of producer Leland Hayward. "Well, no marriage is perfect," Slim said. It never occurred to her to take Pam seriously as a threat. Big, big mistake. While Slim was traveling, Pam circled. Hayward liked to be taken care of, and Pam happily brought his slippers. "Is she beautiful?" Hayward's daughter asked. Well, no, he said. He said he was captivated by Pam's "extraordinary attention span." Helpfully, Pam quoted box office receipts, cooked her man chicken hash on the road, and created "paradise at home." He let Slim go without regrets.

Married to Harriman, Pam took up bridge, the Democratic party, and his interest in the Soviet Union. His Washington power base grew through "issue dinners" she threw. As a birthday present, by golly, she became an American citizen. Before he slipped off to bed at night, Harriman found his favorite flower lying on crisp sheets. He said that marrying Pam was "the best decision" he ever made. No kidding.

After Harriman's death, Pam put her great wealth behind Bill Clinton's 1992 bid for President, and was made Ambassador to France in return. She snowed the French instantly—how else?—by getting an immediate grasp of the issues and putting them at the center of the world. Asked if she'd had a happy life, she said, "Very, very. I drank deep of the well." She died at the Paris Ritz after swimming laps in the pool.

Pamela's Lesson

Pamela was proof that the seductive arts can be learned. She did it (much the way you are now) by soaking up the lessons of the greats and assessing her particular strengths. As a girl, Pam was fascinated by Sirens such as Lady Randolph Churchill (Winston's mother), Emma Hamilton (the mistress of Admiral Nelson), and the great courtesans of long ago. Later, she befriended the Duchess of Windsor who, no beauty herself, had famously robbed England of its King. Pam carefully emulated the Duchess's "anticipation of the Duke's every need and adoption of his every interest," surpassing her mentor in zeal. Pam had her men believing they were masters of the universe—or at least of the universe she was in.

Pam claimed her high-placed conquests were never by design but a happy accident. Don't believe a word of it. In wartime London, Pam wouldn't give a soldier the time of day unless he had a rank of considerable consequence. When she saw something she liked, she dove—and believe me, he was never without a sizable bank account. From Aly Khan, a world-class womanizer, she learned the technique of concentrating her whole attention on one conquest at a time, even when someone more important walked into a room.

"I don't think she is ever truly happy without a man in her life," said Pam's son Winston. In fact, she was quite lost. Being a Siren was the foundation of her whole sense of self. "When Pamela met a man she adored," said a friend, "she just unconsciously assumed his identity." For Fiat heir Agnelli, she turned Catholic and spoke in an Italian accent. For French banking scion Rothschild, she became an expert on the family vineyards, art, and eighteenth-century furniture. Moving from Agnelli to Rothschild, she changed her telephone greeting from *"Pronto!"* to *"Ici,* Pam." She baffled friends during a game of charades when she couldn't come up with English words. She lavished on men "geisha-like" attentions that included, it was rumored, expert sex she didn't much care for herself.

"A beautiful woman is one I notice," said John Erskine, "a charming woman is one who notices me." Had Pam been more beautiful, we might be down one seductress. Charm is partly a talent for concentrating on others—and the technique is by no means exclusive to the Mother or Companion Siren. You don't need to adopt his religion, or nationality, or jump into his skin, but even in moderation, a little Pamela can be a marvelous thing. It's true what they say: men (and not just men) seek to be validated. Few can resist unconditional love when it comes their way. I've seen Sirens succeed through devotion—if not at first, then over the long term.

"PAMELIZE" THEM

"The way a cowboy and a fine horse could cut a steer out from a herd for branding," Pam singled a man out in the crowd. Sitting down with him for five or ten minutes, she focused on what he'd been doing, how he felt—talking in her "throaty, conspiratorial whisper" that said, "this is just between us." She concentrated on "making him shine" and feel comfortable—always the strength of a Companion Siren. Then she would repeat the process with someone else—though needless to say, never a woman. The "full-frontal treatment," "heady" for men, came to be known as being "Pamelized."

Make it your job to be present, focusing gently when he speaks. Don't just look, really *see* him. In conversation, sharpen your listening skills—like Pam, hang on to his every word. Throw him your adoring look. It shouldn't be that hard, just let him see how you feel by the smoldering look in your eyes. Guide the talk to his interests, and ask questions that allow him to boast. With the skill of a great courtesan (or diplomat) make him feel that, even if just for tonight, he might well be the axis on which the sun rises and sets. When next you see him, follow up on that tricky situation he mentioned he's taken on in the Mideast. Offer up that tidbit on spelunking (his passion) you found on the Internet.

Like Pamela, focus your full concentration on a man, one at a time—don't let your eyes stray from him to the man across the room. Let him know that you've always seen things from his marvelous point of view. Don't use the time to talk about yourself *ad nauseam*. Never gossip about one man with the next. Lavish attentions from a Siren such as you are likely to be returned gratefully. If not, do as Pam did. Move on.

make him laugh

CASE STUDY:

Carole Lombard

(née Jane Alice Peters)

1908–1942

Companion Siren

During the golden era of Hollywood, the multi-millionaire Jock Whitney threw a formal afternoon party at which guests were asked to wear white only. "Those society mucky-mucks," said actress Carole Lombard. "They think of all kinds of craziness"—but Lombard was wackier still. Poking fun at the event's formality, she got her doctor to loan her a white hospital gown and wrapped herself in a white mask and bandages. She pulled into the party in an ambulance with sirens blaring and was carried in on a stretcher by two interns. Guests rushed to the scene and found Lombard laughing uproariously. The gag hooked Clark Gable, who knew the actress from *No Man of Her Own*, a picture they had starred in a few years before. Within the week, the duo was Hollywood's golden couple— Brangelina, except with a raucous sense of humor.

Beautiful, blonde, zany Carole Lombard virtually invented the "screwball" comedy, the Depression era's answer to the slapstick romance. The films introduced a new brand of heroine—the smart, sassy, madcap dame who ran circles around men who were essentially clueless. In her more than forty films, Lombard played everything from a gold-digging manicurist in *Hands Across the Table* and a ditzy debutante in *My Man Godfrey*, to a movie queen in her standout film, *Twentieth Century*. As audiences came to learn, Lombard was not so far in real life from the girl in the movies who blithely stopped traffic dead in its tracks to search for a quarter that had rolled across the street.

Jane Alice Peters was born in Fort Wayne, Indiana—hence, her nickname,

"The Hoosier Tornado." After her parents divorced, Lombard's mother moved the kiddies to Hollywood. Lombard was discovered while playing softball in the street and was cast in her first film, *A Perfect Crime*, at age twelve. Her brothers taught their kid sister to swear like a sailor, and Lombard's salty speech would become one of her trademarks. At sixteen, she won a contract with Fox but was dropped when her face was seriously scarred in a car accident. A few years later, she fought her way back—as a screwball comedienne.

"I live by a man's code, designed to fit a man's world, yet at the same time I never forget that a woman's first job is to choose the right shade of lipstick."

—*Carole Lombard*

"Audiences loved Lombard because she promised laughs and always delivered them," wrote a biographer. The same could be said of her co-stars. She didn't have the heart for the rebuff—except, apparently, when it came to the producer Harry Cohn. "Look, Mr. Cohn, I've agreed to be in your shitty little picture," she said, "but fucking you is no part of the deal." He adjusted his pants and insisted that she use his first name. Lombard turned legions of suitors— George Raft, Gary Cooper, and writer Robert Riskin, among them—into "sexy friendships," though they never gave up hoping for more. On set, she was the beloved team player, blowing her lines to make inexperienced actors feel at home.

"Her entry on a set often occasions so many greetings from propmen, mechanics, assistant directors, and electricians on the rafters," noted *Life* magazine, "that the uproar sounds like a reunion between Tarzan and his monkeys." During the shooting of *From Heaven to Hell*, Lombard shivered in a summer dress in the middle of January. "All right you warm, bloody bastards," she joked, "every one of you (get) down to your jockey shorts!" They stripped.

When Lombard fell for a man, she fell hard, happily morphing into whatever they asked of her. "I was the best fuckin' wife you ever saw," said Lombard about her marriage to actor William Powell. She brushed up on her literary skills, kept house, took care of his clothes, and was "a ladylike wife. Because that's how Philo (Powell) wanted it"—though Harriet Nelson I'm sure she was not. Powell wanted her to give up her career, but after two years they shucked the marriage instead. For Clark Gable, she turned herself inside out.

"Lombard was a lesson to all women," said actress Esther Williams. "She didn't like hunting or fishing but she went with him anyway," in safari wear, mind you, which she had cut to make her look like a fashion plate. She bested Gable at sport. "I've got to hold back. I can shoot like a sonofabitch y'know," she told a friend. How like a Companion Siren to take the back seat for the man she loves. For their first Valentine's Day, Lombard sent Gable a dilapidated Model-T Ford covered with hearts. The gift spoofed Gable's passionate interest in vintage automobiles. He picked her up in it for a joy ride, and they partied all night. The rest is romantic history. "They had an ineffable quality in romance," said Williams, "the ability to have fun together. They were soul mates who thought life was delicious. . . ."

After a long courtship, Gable and Lombard married. Three years later, her plane smacked into a mountainside when she was returning to California from a trip east to promote WWII bonds. Gable married twice again but was never the same. He is buried next to his screwball girl.

ACQUAINT THEM WITH THE LADY FROM NANTUCKET

You don't have to be a comedienne to tell a good joke. Just don't stumble in your delivery, and practice, of course, will make it perfect. As long as you're at it, why not make it a raunchy one? Guys love the off-color joke, but they don't expect a woman to tell it well. When she does, it has the titillating whiff of the forbidden. They're a little shocked, confused, but also turned on.

She was dropped by Fox. It looked like curtains for the film career. But the car accident that seriously scarred Lombard's face actually proved to be the making of the screwball girl. It was "the beginning," said a friend, "of her philosophy, her inner life. For she began to laugh at herself—and she went on laughing at herself for as long as she lived." That *joie* was so infectious, it drew Gable from across the room. "For some reason this got to ol' Clark," she said of her entrance at Jock Whitney's white-only afternoon party. "He thought it was hot stuff," though she didn't quite understand it herself. "We worked together and did all kinds of love scenes and everything," she said about co-starring with Gable in *No Man of Her Own*. "And I never got any kind of tremble out of him." Gable was apparently drawn to the comedienne in her.

Lombard's humor came down to a profound irreverence—and the need to tweak convention wherever she saw it. She couldn't resist poking fun at those who

The doors come with.

took themselves too seriously. She threw a Roman banquet when friends groused that they were too tired to sit up. Their health complaints inspired a "hospital bash" with cocktails that were served in test tubes. When a movie of Gable's bombed everywhere but China, she dropped aerial leaflets printed with, "Fifty Million Chinamen Can't Be Wrong!" She teased Gable about his frugality, large ears, and "the greater popularity of Shirley Temple." Lombard's screwball view helped him laugh at the world.

If you're knock-down, drag-out funny, chances are you already know it. And when it comes to wit, you either have it or you don't. Nothing short of a brain transplant will make it otherwise. But you *develop* a sense of humor through your way of looking at the world. Like Lombard, you can start by seeing the world as a funnier place—and by remembering that you're neither the second coming nor the elusive cure for baldness. Actively seek out what's odd, colorful, or a hoot in the everyday. Then ask what you'd add to the mix to make it goofier still. Just lost your last dime down a subway grate? See the humor in your predicament, and make a funny story out of it. Try going in for the gag—say, by showing up at a garden party dressed as a "ho." Once you got the hang of it, you be takin' the screwball point of view.

Screwball is a state of mind, a kind of kooky optimism backed up by a lot of nerve. It thrives on the self-deprecating joke and a feel for the absurd. Diane Keaton, Rita Rudner, and Teri Garr are all irresistibly funny women whose humor is based on self-mockery. If you can remain charmingly oblivious of the effect—one of Lombard's bits—it's better still. But resist the urge to self-destruct by bringing down the house with your imitation of the uptight waiter at your boss's upscale holiday party. By all means, make a joke at your own expense. If you can do it with a lampshade on your head—well . . . don't.

Laugh easily and often. You'd be surprised how often the good laugher is credited with wit. If you sound like a hyena, try to keep it to more of a titter. If you don't get funnier day by day, at least you'll be a happier person to be with. It made Carole Lombard positively irresistible. The Siren who's high on life is always unfailingly popular.

be brilliant in conversation

Veronica Franco

1546–1591

Companion Siren

When the twenty-three-year-old King of France passed through Venice in the summer of 1574, the city swung into high gear trying to impress him. He was carried in a ship rowed by four-hundred oarsmen. He passed under an arch made by Palladio and painted with ornate flourishes by the artists Veronese and Titian. Spectacles included a marine monster breathing fire from a furnace, meals of 1,200 items served on silver plates, and an opera written for the occasion, along with an array of balls, theater pieces, musical presentations, and dancing girls. But this was just the beginning of the wooing of Henri III. He was presented with the *Catalogue of the Chief and Most Renowned Courtesans of Venice*—a visitor's guide to illicit sex—and he studied dozens of little portraits carefully. He chose Veronica Franco, the city's treasure, and was spirited away to her by gondola. He spent the evening with Veronica discussing literature and making love, and returned at daybreak with her portrait and sonnets comparing him to Zeus.

At the end of the sixteenth century, Venice was a city of 100,000 citizens, with 11,654 of them prostitutes. They draped themselves across gondolas and exposed their ample bosoms from balconies and windows. A kind of X-rated Disneyland, Renaissance Venice was a tourist destination, thanks in large part to the thrills of their wanton women. The difference between a prostitute and a courtesan could be measured by the quality of her company. Unlike aristocratic women, courtesans were educated and prided themselves on their eloquence. Their noble clients sought escape in conversation that went beyond the variables of weather.

Veronica Franco was a legendary beauty—her peaked brow and full lips were recorded in living color by Tintoretto. Given the breadth of the competition, her sexual skills would have been beyond reproach. But Veronica distinguished herself as an "honest courtesan"—one whose reputation was made outside the bedroom. Under the patronage of Domenico Venier, the intellectual kingpin of Venice, Veronica became a published poet, part of his elect salon of writers and thinkers. When Venice needed a political ally in the King of France, Veronica was an essential part of the full court press—a woman who could charm a man on so many levels, he could be pushed where she chose. In the Hollywood film version, *Dangerous Beauty*, Henri's visit with Franco closed the deal on a fleet of ships. The truth is a little sketchier. But let's just say Henri's time with Veronica didn't hurt Venice a bit.

"Eloquence in a woman leads to promiscuity," is a line plucked from *Dangerous Beauty*. Conversation was considered so potentially seductive in sixteenth-century Venice that aristocratic women were effectively muzzled, locked away by their husbands behind gilded doors. Talk attracts attention, was the prevailing wisdom. A lady who attracts attention runs the risk of making a mistake and compromising her lily-white reputation—or worse. As Franco's movie mother explains, "desire begins in the mind." If you need further proof, a Venetian courtesan charged one price for "the whole deal," and separately just for the sheer erotic pleasure of speaking with her.

"In the manner of the Japanese geisha," wrote Franco's biographer, the courtesan was expected to be "an educated and skillful conversationalist and an entertainer of men"—an artful Companion Siren. In her hands, conversation was a consensual act of heightened sensitivity to her partner's interests and moods. Her goal was to transport him away from cares of the everyday and into a pleasure zone. "Thou must fortifie thine eares against the attractive enchantments of their plausible speeches," warned a traveler to Venice. More than four hundred years later, the name Veronica Franco survives owing to the seductive power of her words.

In good times, sixteenth-century Venetians flaunted their courtesans, the ultimate luxury item. In bad, these women became convenient scapegoats. Veronica was called up before the Inquisition on charges of "magical incantations" after the plague decimated the city in the mid-1570s. She successfully defended herself with clever rhetoric. Sadly, the city's "recognized mistress of speech" died of a fever while she was still quite young, but evidence of her eloquence survives in her published words.

Veronica's Lesson

"The ideal of conversation, which managed to marry lightheartedness with depth, elegance with pleasure, and the search for truth with a tolerant respect for the opinions of others, has never lost its appeal," writes Benedetta Craveri in *The Age of Conversation*. I'm totally with her on this, but isn't it getting hard to pull off these days? Surely you've been a guest at dinner parties where everyone talks at once. Or on a date that feels like a Senate filibuster? How about the gathering where a few are glued to the television or Internet—or worse, the cell phone. What ever happened to leisurely conversation, that great give-and-take, where folks talked without fear of being cut off? "The opposite of talking isn't listening," says writer Fran Lebowitz, "it's waiting your turn." Get ready to be the Siren who brings back conversation as a seduction tool.

STOP, LOOK, AND LISTEN

"Being interested generally makes one interesting," says Barbara Walters in *How to Talk with Practically Anyone About Practically Anything*, which outlines a three-pronged approach:

✦ *Stop.* Do your homework; know as much about the situation as you possibly can.

✦ *Look.* Give the person you're with the flattery of your total attention. The most charming people I know give the impression that they've waited all day to speak to me alone.

✦ *Listen.* Don't *pretend* to be listening—but *really* listen.

Who would know better than Barbara, the woman who's talked to everyone?

What makes a seductive conversationalist? Would that we could consult Veronica Franco directly. *The Age of Conversation*—which covers the art at its seventeenth-century height in France—mentions curiosity as key. As a girl, Veronica gobbled up the crumbs of learning left behind by her brothers and their tutors. That avid curiosity, forbidden to women, led her to consume books on the sly, meaning she was better prepped to engage with men of the world. Yet, in its heyday, conversation "made no display of learning . . . avoided quotations, examples, and proverbs." In the right hands, it was a contact high, a kind of sublime foreplay. It "radiated a soothing oblivion," creating an atmosphere of "relaxation, entertainment, and instruction." The best conversations were orchestrated not so one tiresome bore could hold forth but to draw each person out in turn. The secret of a brilliant conversationalist was this: she was interested in what others had to say.

There's nothing quite as seductive as someone who "is endlessly fascinated by people," confirms Barbara Walters, a conversational Siren herself, in *How to Talk with Practically Anyone About Practically Anything*. Rich, poor, old, young—she "wants to know how they live, what they eat, how they feel about themselves sexually." Can *you* resist the person who sincerely wants to know more about *you*? Centuries ago, in the famed salons of Sirens like Madame de Staël and the Marquise de Rambouillet, the talented conversationalist prided herself on her intuitive feel for the person with whom she conversed. Going further, she used a Socratic form of questioning designed to bring out stellar qualities in her partner, perhaps unrealized even by himself. In the twenty-first century, this is what Madame Walters might call "doing your homework." Get to know everything about the man you're talking to.

"Conversation . . . demanded total spontaneity, an open, cheerful face, a natural, affable manner, an expression of interest and expectation . . . in the seventeenth century." I couldn't have said it better myself, so I won't. Similarly, Walters cites warmth as the most consistently endearing quality, second only to wit—particularly at your own expense—as unfailingly sexy. She offers a caveat: don't make the adolescent mistake of trying to impress a man by insulting him.

And, finally, all importantly, there's listening. In the age of conversation, a talent for listening was more prized than one for speaking—astonishing to hear in the age of the squeaky wheel.

USE HIS NAME

It's such a small and flattering technique, but few seem to be able to make the effort to do it. Always remember names and use them. "I was so hoping I'd see you here tonight, Lionel! (delighted pause) It will give me the opportunity I've wanted to catch up with you." It shows that you are fully tuned in. "Using his name is a little like touching, but safer," says my Competitor Siren friend Samantha. Be careful not to overdo, lest he suspect you've got some swampland in Florida you need to unload.

Don't be the Siren who only talks about the adorable antics of your dog, or the foods permitted on your new diet. Be a woman of the world, the seductress who can talk about anything. Expand on subjects, but don't belabor them. And never make a point of calling attention to how smart and accomplished you are. Seductive conversation is the art of bringing others out, not an audition for a reality show. In getting to know him, don't ask him what his company's profits are. Walters suggests giving your questions more of an intimate twist: "Can you describe the moment you first realized you were good at what you do?" Aside from sex, there's no more seductive way to connect.

The Siren who disagrees does so with humor and humility. She shows the utmost respect for his opinions, even when he's a Republican and she's not. When you're in a conversational fix, do as Barbara Walters does—look receptive by reenacting "the most luminous, loving you." Make eye contact, give him your undivided attention, and laugh at his jokes. Show interest in whatever turns him on. Misery isn't good company, by the way. Make your complaints on your own time.

learn to cook

Nigella Lawson

1960–

Sex Kitten/Mother Siren

With a come-hither look, Nigella Lawson leads you into her pantry. Like the chef herself, it's replete, lush, full of tasty surprises—"yummy," as she says often and with feeling. On *Nigella's Feasts*, her Food Network show, she whips up a meal with an abandon approaching recklessness. Afterwards, her perspective on food lingers like a first kiss. Who knew food was so sexy, until Nigella—in a frock that would be prim if it weren't so tight—had a go at it. She licks icing off a spoon with a little more tongue than seems decent, and actually moans on contact with a lamb glaze. And who can forget the interesting way Nigella has of testing linguini: dangling the noodle Roman orgy-style over her up-raised lips. "I call it gastroporn," she says. "Food exists in the realm of the senses. . . . I like to make an intimate connection with my viewers and readers."

Before Nigella, it was fashionable to shun your inner domestic goddess—a persona that we identified with Ethel Mertz. Cooking without a million-dollar kitchen and exotic ingredients was housework. A man's heart could only be reached through starving yourself and frequent trips to the gym, or so we were told by post-feminists. "It is impossible to convey the pleasure of eating, the real voluptuous joy to be gotten out of food," Nigella wrote in *How to Eat*, her first cookbook, "if we don't feel that joy ourselves." Forget the gym, forget the complicated meals cooked to perfection, says Nigella. Just serve it up simple from the kitchen.

Aptly, Lawson is potboiler beautiful—with long, dark tresses, twinkling eyes, and creamy skin. Her voluptuous form proves that what she preaches, she practices. She was born in England with a silver mixing spoon in those ruby lips. Her

father was Margaret Thatcher's Chancellor of the Exchequer, and her mother, a glamorous socialite. At age twenty-nine, Nigella married John Diamond, a fellow *Sunday Times* columnist, but their charmed life would be cut short. Diamond died of cancer, but not before he encouraged Nigella to write cookbooks for women who entered their kitchens with fear and loathing. Her voluptuous voice came out in bestsellers like *How to Eat*, *Nigella Bites*, and *Feast*. She's now married to the art dealer Charles Saatchi, who begs her not to lose her extra pounds.

"Cooking is not just about applying heat, procedure, method," writes Lawson in her cookbook *Forever Summer*, "but about transformation of a more intimate kind." In the words of *Newsweek*, is this *Joy of Sex* or *Joy of Cooking* we're talking about? She prescribes heavy chopping as foreplay—a way of "loosening up" before making something "that can seduce people." She manages to work words like "masturbation" and "ruptured hymen" into cookbook text in a way that seems not only natural, but appropriate. With every dollop of Sex Kitten, Nigella folds in heaping tablespoons of a Mother Siren's solicitousness. You have no trouble imagining her feeding chicken soup to the feverish. What Nigella aims to revive is comfort food. Her tasty recipes are homey, the kind your mother surely would have made if she'd cooked.

"Noël Coward wrote that it was strange how potent cheap music can be; the same—in a different sphere— holds true in the kitchen."

—*Nigella Lawson*, Feast

"For a baby, food and intimacy are inextricably linked," writes Nigella, "and that connection never goes away." Lemon chicken and mash aside, she offers truth in food: if the way to a man's heart is through his stomach, it's because that's how he's hardwired in the womb. As surely as he loves the mother who fed him, he'll fall for the Siren who cooks. "A hot woman who loves to eat and knows the way to a man's heart is hard to resist," notes AskMen.com about Nigella. It's time to rethink our relationship to the home-cooked meal.

Nigella's Lesson

Back in the Fifties, Betty Crocker offered recipes called "Beau-Catchers and Husband Keepers." She advised that cooking from anything other than scratch would ruin a woman's marital health. Tired of being slaves in the kitchen, women extinguished their pilot lights. Then came gourmet cooking—as nerve-wracking as preparing for the LSAT. "One of the greatest hindrances to enjoying cooking is that tense-necked desire to impress others," writes Nigella in *How to Eat*. Who needs the pressure of being a Picasso with a basting brush? Nothing is quite so off-putting as the hostess who greets her guests at the door on the verge of nervous collapse. "Remember that it is not a test of your worth and acceptability. It's just dinner," she says. Still, "just dinner" can be a powerful turn-on.

According to *USA Today*, forty-five percent of Americans still believe that the way to a man's heart is through a meal, and more than twenty-five percent report success in using home cooking to serve their amorous purposes. Burnished in my memory is a picture of my father kissing my mother's hand in elaborate thanks for her transcendent *steak au poivre*—which, by the way, is little more than steak with pepper, set on fire in a frying pan. He was joking, of course, but not entirely. A friend of mine claimed she could induce marriage proposals through her recipes. I scoffed—loudly. She had the last laugh when she married one of my beaus out from under my nose. Too late, I guess, to ask for the ingredients?

More than ever, cooking is a Siren's secret weapon. Because cooking is less of an everyday event, it is idealized—the woman who can pull off a meatloaf is virtually a heroine in his eyes. It's so much easier than we've been led to believe. "Men like simple food," says Nigella. "Not fussy sauces or fancy restaurant fare, but good food, cooked plainly, but well." Check with Pamela Churchill (later

Harriman), who found her way into theater producer Leland Hayward's heart by cooking him chicken hash on the road. Tasty food makes a man happy. It can transport him from being irritable to feeling satisfied.

"Try to come up with his idea of a perfect meal, no matter how basic or unglamorous," says Nigella. But that doesn't mean you have to cook something you hate. A meal you both can't happily share is no good. Ease yourself into a limited repertoire—a simple roast chicken, a leg of lamb, braised pork tenderloin. If you're always cooking something new or exotic, you'll never master the fundamentals you need to improve your skills. A dandy place to start is Nigella's *How to Eat*, or one of the perennial classics like *Joy of Cooking*. Don't think of a roast as another hunk of meat. Bond with your dish and make it yours.

SLIP A LITTLE SOMETHING EXTRA IN

The Indian asparagus dish *shodavari*—translated as "one hundred marriages"—apparently boosts a woman's sexiest hormones. But before you go combing the gourmet shops, consider that Cleopatra swore by figs and Napoleon dipped into the truffle box. A short list of aphrodisiacs includes everything from ginseng to yohimbe, rose petals, chili peppers, herring, honey, pomegranates, prawns, lobster, oysters, lampreys, walnuts, wild orchid nectar, dates, cardamom, coriander, cumin, ginger, saffron, clove, cinnamon, garlic, chocolate, and horseradish.

"Paint the canvas," which Nigella claims is "curiously relaxing"—flowers on the table, a pot boiling on the stove, with you as the Siren in the middle of it all. Dip into the chaos, she says. "Learn to live with stains and spills." When Nigella separates an egg, it looks like she's trying to get it all over herself. That doesn't mean you should sit down to dinner looking like you need a bib. Cooking should be "relaxed, expansive, authentic—it should reflect your personality," not your five-year plan. Emphasize plenty. It's better to be packing leftovers than to look ungenerous. Like Nigella, praise your ingredients for their staggering good looks. There's nothing wrong with flirting with food.

In time, anyone can master a few recipes and get them on the table without falling apart. What will distinguish you is your attitude. To quote Nigella: "Food isn't just love, food encompasses everything." It's how we celebrate everything from a holiday to his release from jail. As the chef, you are "the provider of good things and the person who gives an essential embrace." Show your abashed appreciation of food not just in the way you cook but in the way you eat. It's as important to feel like a Domestic Goddess as it is to be one.

Art for Alma's sake . . .

be a muse

Alma Mahler Gropius Werfel

(née Schindler)

1879–1964

Sex Kitten/Goddess Siren

"If you don't soon become my wife my great talent will come to a miserable end," the artist Oskar Kokoschka wrote in 1914. "We seek each other, want each other, must have each other so that destiny . . . can be fulfilled." In her own sweet time, Alma delivered her verdict. "I will marry you when you have produced a master-piece!" Kokoschka bartered with a painting of a couple tossed by raging seas in a giant cockleshell. A woman, Alma, sleeps on the shoulder of her lover, Kokoschka, who looks haunted by something other than his strange and watery predicament. *The Tempest* or *Bride of the Wind*, an acknowledged masterpiece, hangs in Basel's Kunstmuseum today.

Alma Schindler was "irresistible and irresistibly attracted to original men." Or as she wrote in her memoirs, "God granted me the privilege of knowing the brilliant works of our time, before they left the hands of their creators." Her romantic dilemma was never "Who do I love?" but "Who's more likely to create the greater work of art?" In choosing the fortyish Gustav Mahler for a husband, Alma suffered gambler's remorse. "What if Alex becomes famous?" she wondered of Mahler's rival for her love. "Would it be possible for you, from now on, to regard *my* music as *yours*?" Mahler wrote nineteen-year-old Alma. Done.

The daughter of a landscape painter, Alma Schindler was thrown into Vienna's society of Secessionist artists at an early age. She was fascinated by talent; her first romance was with the painter Gustav Klimt, an older ladies man. In her family, a catastrophe would have been marriage to a "worthless moneyed" person. Alma was torn: should she pursue what she felt was her own calling to be great, or become the muse to a star? In creative bursts, she composed *Lieder* (German ballads). But the romantic attentions of famous men proved so gratifying to her ego that she became a collector instead, assembling geniuses like winter coats. After Mahler's death, she married the Bauhaus architect Walter Gropius, then divorced him for the writer Franz Werfel. She inspired enough works to fill a gallery.

NEED TO KNOW DEPT.

Dumped by Alma, what did that wacky artist Oskar Kokoschka do? He commissioned a life-sized doll, whose proportions matched Alma's, down to her dainty fingernails. Kokoschka christened his doll "the silent woman" and took her everywhere, dressed to the nines in clothes from Paris that Alma might have chosen herself. The silent woman met her end when Kokoschka decapitated her in a public square.

Artists are never in short supply, but a gifted muse is as rare as a celebrity sighting in Wichita. Would Mahler have created his Sixth or Eighth symphonies without his muse to turn him on? Deprived of "the light of my life," he claimed he would "have gone out like a torch deprived of air." Werfel praised Alma's "sibylline vantage point." It was she who spurred the poet, notoriously lazy, to write the novel *The Forty Days of Musa Dagh*, his first substantial success. "She is there as a power," he wrote, "as a productive organism . . . who has really acquired great influence over me." She transported her men to a higher level of creativity.

Of the century's great Sirens, few could rival Alma Mahler, and nothing could disrupt her unshakeable conviction that she was the center of the world. Alma never worried that *they* would fall out of love; she assumed, quite rightly, that she'd be the one to leave. Rare was the artist who didn't propose to Alma within a week, or who didn't suffer tortures when she'd gone. "You must revive me at night," demanded Kokoschka, "like a magic potion." Sex was the restorative font for their creativity, and her judgment the final word.

FLAUNT YOUR SKILLS

Never modest about her input, Alma displayed her trophies. Under a glass case in her living room was Gustav Mahler's Tenth Symphony, open to the composer's notes to her scrawled across the page. Kokoschka's celebrated painting of Alma as Lucrezia Borgia hung on the wall. As a muse, remember that modesty is not a virtue; it will only ensure that your contribution will be overlooked. Think of his work as yours. After all, where would he be without your input?

"I never really liked Mahler's music. I was never interested in what Werfel wrote," concluded Alma. Gropius's architecture was of no interest. The Goddess routinely raised them up, only to knock them off their pedestals. "But, Kokoschka, yes Kokoschka always impressed me." Ironic, isn't it? Dressed in perpetual black and living in New York, Alma would become Mahler's professional widow. She organized his papers, wrote *her* memoirs, and complained about the deplorable lack of material to interest a muse. "There are so few . . . Leonard Bernstein. Thornton Wilder. It is not as it used to be."

Alma's Lesson

Is a talented muse the product of nature, nurture, or force of will? And doesn't a muse have to be beautiful? It depends on what kind of muse you intend to be: a creative partner or one who poses prettily. The twentieth century's other busy muse—Lou Andreas-Salomé—had Rilke, Nietzsche, and Freud eating out of her hand through her deeply seductive understanding of their work, though it's said that her nose might have served as a float. Alma's "pretty features led one to expect her to say silly, obvious things," a biographer wrote, "and nothing of this sort ever passed her lips." She devoured Nietzsche like candy, and could discuss art, literature, and theology. For fun, she played entire Wagner operas on the piano. Her Mama didn't raise no fool, and it turned them on.

"Her perception is sharp and clear," wrote Werfel. "I believe in her judgments, good and bad, especially the bad." Mahler's symphonies always passed through Alma before they were offered to an orchestra. But no one valued Alma's opinion more than Alma herself. On meeting a man she deemed exceptional, she "exalted his gifts." Together they drank deeply from her creative well. "Everything about him is holy to me. I would like to kneel before him & kiss his loins—kiss everything, everything," she wrote. I don't need to tell *you* what's going on here. "Each of my meetings with Alma," claimed Mahler, "gives me renewed energy for my work." Sex and art, art and sex? You can see how the two became confused.

> "Whenever a gifted male artist has embraced his Muse he has in fact made a woman appear in the art. . . . It is not the man speaking through the woman; it is the woman speaking through the man."
>
> —*Arlene Croce*

Is that half-written novel taking up space in your underwear drawer? Do people rush at your paintings with sponges, mistaking them for accidents? Don't despair. A critic once said about Alma, "I can assure you that we would never have heard of her" if her reputation had depended on her songs alone. Perhaps you've always considered art a sacred language and artists worthy of elaborate worship. Consider channeling all that creative energy into becoming a muse. So thoroughly did Alma believe in her power to ignite masterpieces that artists believed it themselves. And in the Siren world, it's the believing that makes it true.

Your first order is to present yourself as a kind of Simon Cowell—but with more of the delivery of Paula Abdul. If you can't make it smart, it's better to close your mouth, look discerning, and say nothing at all. Few could beat Alma for the

diss that made them realize they were dealing with someone formidable. When Mahler sent over his *Lieder* for her to see, she suggested he peruse some excellent writings on silence by the intellectual Maeterlinck. A caveat: without great sex, you won't be a muse. You'll be nothing more than his worst critic.

He "let me feel his masculinity—his vigor—& it was pure, holy sensation," Alma wrote in her diaries. She longed to be raped, plundered, pillaged, and possessed, and said so in no uncertain terms. Alma oozed sex; she was keenly alive to the sensual. Ye gads, she was only nineteen, and this was the close of the Victorian years. Then and now, the muse's power ultimately depends on her bounteous sexuality, which Alma was also willing to withhold if need be. Werfel and Kokoschka were banished until they got up to speed, and the result was their abundant creativity. "There is one person on earth who can bring me fulfillment and make an artist of me," Werfel wrote Alma. "You are that person."

PRACTICE YOUR UNFLINCHING GAZE

Lady Caroline Blackwood—the "dangerous muse" of the 1960s—also worshipped talent, drew from the "well-spring of sex," and was notoriously difficult to please. Lady Caroline's signature? An unflinching stare, paired with eerie silence. By artists, that gaze was interpreted as judgment—rarely good. Lady Caroline was married successively to the artist Lucian Freud, the composer Israel Citkowitz, and the Pulitzer Prize-winning poet Robert Lowell, all of whom did their best work with her.

A muse who confuses her Leonardos (DiCaprio, da Vinci) is not a muse—she's really more of a groupie. In short, to be a muse like Alma, you need to have an understanding of the work you hope to inspire. Establish that your good opinion is the prize to be won, and that the spoils you deliver are sinfully sweet. He'll soon understand that his creative juices flow directly from you. Apply romantic compresses of hot and cold. Your love is never unconditional. Keep them yearning in the service of art, and always remember Alma's words: "If I was allowed to assist these knights for a while, then my existence is justified and blessed!"

CAN YOU TRANSPORT THEM?

Do you have the talent to take a man out of himself? Are you the Siren who slays them simply by making them feel good? If "yes" is more often your answer to the questions below, it could be that transporting men is your route to Sirenhood.

+ Are you an optimist?
+ In conversation, do you seek to understand others more than you seek to be understood?
+ Do you get a rush out of making others laugh or feel happy?
+ Are you inclined to not take yourself too seriously?
+ Do you feel that a woman is often capable of seeing and bringing out the best in a man?
+ Do you consider yourself emotionally intelligent or intuitive?
+ Do you feel food can be an effective tool of seduction, as well as a source of nurture?
+ Do you think that laughter is one of the best ways to connect with a man?
+ Are you the kind of person who inspires or brings out the best in others?
+ Do you consider sex to be a creative restorative?
+ Is it your opinion that while men like a challenge, they are most interested in being unconditionally loved?
+ Is eating a voluptuous experience for you?

Lead Them to the Bedroom

Sex. Well, what can I say? For a Siren to be a Siren—make no mistake—sex appeal is requisite. You may look like a Goddess, dressed to kill. Maybe you make them laugh until they ache, or dazzle them as completely as Cleopatra barging down the Nile. But if he's looking at you and not thinking of sex, you might as well hang up your dancing shoes. You've got to lead them to the bedroom and have some idea of what you're doing when you get there.

Inside every Siren beats the heart of a Sex Kitten—which means by a look, a word, or a way of moving, she knows how to draw a man's attention from across the room. Yet, it's the Competitor Sirens who are often innovators in the field. Brandishing a libido that's like a man's, it never occurs to a Competitor Siren not to venture into sexual territory where few have gone before. No matter what kind of Siren you are, you should feel free to travel there yourself.

Even when it's bad, it's good, as the expression goes. But when it's forbidden, it's out of this world. Leave it to Angelina Jolie for lessons on how to walk on the wild side, and the writer Colette for the switch hit. Mae West mastered the art of talking dirty, without actually saying anything scandalous. Nineteenth-century courtesan Cora Pearl set the erotic stage with unusual creativity. Did Catherine the Great actually make love to her horse? Or was she just a particularly randy Empress? Read on, and you'll know all.

set the erotic stage

CASE STUDY:

Cora Pearl

(née Emma Crouch)

1835–1886

Competitor Siren

On an evening in Paris more than a century ago, Cora Pearl was entertaining her male admirers over dinner when she excused herself. She slipped into the kitchen, dropped her clothes, and carefully arranged her beautiful body on a massive silver serving dish. Her chef, the renowned Salé, decorated her "naked body with rosettes and swathes of creams and sauces," she wrote in her memoirs, "with that deftness and artistry for which he is so famed." Placing a single grape in the hollow of her navel, he surrounded her with meringues and finished her off with a liberal dusting of powdered sugar. Two footmen carried the covered dish in and ceremoniously lifted the lid. There, as we know, was the delectable Pearl.

You won't be surprised to hear that our Siren was not a leading pillar of French society, but in mid-nineteenth-century Paris, no courtesan was more sought after than Cora Pearl. She had come by the profession in the way women of that time often did: as a teenaged and innocent Emma Crouch in her native London, she was lured by a stranger with promises of cake, then drugged, and "ruined." No longer respectable, Emma Crouch became Cora Pearl. Using the money the stranger had left for her, she moved up into the *demimonde* of courtesans. Prince Napoleon and the Duc de Rivoli were among her devoted conquests. Through them, she attained the courtesan's highest ideal: to be kept in a style that makes the word "royal" look pale. Cora's black pearls, "of phenomenal price," were her signature.

"I swear it is a success I never understood," an observer wrote of Cora. "It existed but nothing justifies it." She had "the head of a factory worker," by one unflattering account, a "clown's head," by another. Emile Zola used Cora as a model for the courtesan Lucy Stewart in his novel *Nana*. Like Cora, Lucy's manner and tremendous chic obscured that she was plain "to the point of ugliness"—though Cora's exquisite physique would have made Pamela Anderson's body look like chopped liver. With her talent for erotic theater, she created ways to show that asset at its best, and made herself eminently desirable.

Cora prided herself on avoiding "blind passion and fatal attraction"—the secret of her success. "I have never belonged to anybody. My independence was all my fortune," she said. Without any attachment to one man, the Competitor was free to give herself to many and to extract fees so high they were sometimes ruinous. Boyish, naturally athletic, often coarse, Cora had the Competitor Siren's lusty libido. She cooked up a veritable "acme of sensual delights" beginning with the creative visual. In ways both subtle and bold, she offered what amounted to an eye-catching sexual tease.

"Sex, for all its greatest practitioners, was not just a physical act, but also a state of mind," wrote one of Cora's biographers. And this state of mind was provoked by everything. Not a single moment or movement was left to chance. The courtesan was the mistress of the erotic detail. Sets, costumes, props, and script all figured in creating the *mise-en-scène* for seduction. Any outing was viewed as an opportunity—Sunday worship being among the most popular. Respectable women burned to know the secrets of the courtesan's allure. Though she officially didn't exist, the courtesan often was called in like a physician for consultation on matters involving seduction.

One young man came to financial ruin keeping Cora. In a desperate bid for attention, he forced his way into her house with a pistol and shot himself, though the bullet might have originally been intended for her. Cora worried more about the stain on her rug than she did about her lover's wounds. He recovered, but her reputation didn't. In the hard times that dogged the rest of her life, she called herself "Cora without the pearls."

Cora's Lesson

A courtesan's life was the study of giving men pleasure of all kinds. Her work began at home, the ultimate lair of luxury. Everything was arranged with coquetry and the epicurean view. Rooms were heavily scented with flowers. Sumptuous decorations included carved and canopied beds, *objets d'art*, and luscious fabrics from around the world. No expense was spared on treats—peacock in aspic, partridge with champagne, an array of desserts (which might even feature the hostess). Setting the erotic stage, regardless of where, required continuous creativity. Cora was constantly pulling a rabbit out of her hat. The competition was stiff.

On any given night at the opera, courtesans were always the riveting subplot. One might stick a distinctly phallic looking dagger in her hair. Another would tuck a rosebud in her bodice "in the daintiest of hollows." Still another might arrange her hair in a ziggurat or dye her locks to match her dress—or array herself in jewels and fashions that would suggest the "ultimate luxury goods." Cora's very walk was "doe-like," and the graceful tilt of her head inspired sighs from men in the balcony. If the occasion didn't exist for display, courtesans manufactured it. As Eve at a fancy dress ball, Cora, it was reported in the papers, was "not concealed by any more garments than were worn by the original apple-eater." Cora, bless her, started the fashion of horseback riding in the Bois de Boulogne—knowing full well the "sheer theatre and erotic power" of a woman astride a horse.

What you now see on the racks of Victoria's Secret is a pale imitation of what courtesans invented first. "Cora and her fellow *demi-mondaines* knew only too well what we tend to forget," wrote a biographer, "that what is mysteriously and enticingly half-wrapped is far more alluring than the clinically bare." The sheer luxury of their undergarments and dressing gowns, it's said, was enough to give a man goose pimples. A courtesan might have a different outfit for each lover in his favorite color with gold-embroidered slippers to match—and the expense was positively astronomical. Cora actually took her lingerie maker to court and got a thousand francs knocked off the bill. It was all an important part of the "artillery" for her *mise-en-scène*. Makes you think twice, doesn't it, about those Hanes that have seen better days?

Perhaps, like Cora, you are a woman of unusual nerve. Serving yourself up naked might get you arrested—but the scandal wouldn't hurt. What's to stop you from throwing a costume party as Aphrodite with your cleavage dangerously exposed? Or riding horseback through Central Park in your sleek jodhpurs (or, more romantically, side-saddle)? An enticing image can be worth more than the overt touch and a thousand words. It will be burned in his memory for years to come. Cora was known to entertain them from a bathtub filled with vintage champagne or to dance a revealing can-can on top of a floor strewn with dozens and dozens of orchids.

Grace, beauty, and theatrics can sex up even the everyday event, as long as you're not thinking of wearing your old sweatpants. A simple trip to the market can set your erotic stage—if you're deliciously dressed as you squeeze the produce or elegantly dip to sign your credit card. At home, at work, or out on the town, always consider lighting, props, and script. The Edwardian Siren Lady Randolph Churchill insisted on using pink light bulbs for their rosy glow. You're not likely to set the erotic stage under fluorescent lights, or while you're duking it out with the guy who just cut in front of you in line. Consider all the activities that might show you at your best. Then orchestrate the means by which you can be seen doing them.

LEARN STRIPTEASE

Sounds camp, but a little private striptease can bring out the beast in a man. For divine inspiration, watch Sophia Loren in the 1963 sizzler *Yesterday, Today and Tomorrow*. Loren trained with professionals at the famed Crazy Horse in Paris, and hit it out of the ballpark. Says Loren: "I smiled at (Marcello) Mastroianni. He smiled at me. And then I let him have it," outfitted in a black lace camisole, garters, and stockings. "Slowly, sensuously, tantalizingly, I removed my clothes, letting each article dangle provocatively in front of his eyes while my body undulated to the throbbing music . . . the interplay, the timing, the sexiness, the carnal thunder (of) my tease set off . . . Marcello"—whose unscripted reaction was to howl like a coyote.

Actress Mae West turned her bedroom into an eighteenth-century den of iniquity, in pale pink brocade and gold-and-white-framed mirrors from floor to ceiling. ("I like to see how I'm doin'.") If you're setting the erotic stage, your boudoir should exude comfort and luxury in a style that becomes you. This doesn't necessarily mean a canopied bed, but at the very least it means a credible mattress and inviting sheets. A profusion of flowers, a soulful tune, and a candle wouldn't hurt, as long as you can make your staging look right for the moment. A contemporary of Cora's slept on black sheets to set off her luminous white skin. How about just getting fabulous lingerie and a negligee to replace that soup-stained t-shirt?

Not a speaking role . . .

take charge in the bedroom

CASE STUDY:

Catherine the Great

(née Sophia Augusta Frederika)

1729–1796

Mother/Competitor Siren

By the fall of 1796, Catherine the Great had ruled Russia for nearly thirty-four years, earning many times over her reputation as an enlightened Empress. But she was not without her eccentricities. As her court well knew, her sexual needs were sometimes hard to meet. She was old, portly, and signs of dropsy were now evident in her face, but her voracious appetites remained unchecked. "I have always loved animals," she wrote in her memoirs. Would she now put that admission to a Herculean test? This, dear Sirens, is where the retelling of the urban legend ends. You've heard that Catherine died crushed by the horse with which she was trying to mate? There's absolutely no truth to it. Catherine collapsed from a stroke and slipped into a coma that November day. But her sexual legend lives on.

How did Catherine the Great come by her reputation for, shall we say, creative sex? Likewise, Cleopatra, Marie Antoinette, and the "Virgin" Queen Elizabeth suffered from rumors so obscene they would make spam e-mailers blush. It's the lot of powerful women who are also desirable. True, Catherine's libido was limitless. But she preferred the robust soldier, young and pretty, to lovers with hooves. Even at the end of her life, "the two Zubov brothers and their friend Saltykov took turns with the Czarina in an office . . . vast and . . . difficult to fill." Had her name been Caesar, this wouldn't even have been notable.

"I like to praise and reward in a loud voice and to scold in a whisper."

—Catherine the Great's motto

Catherine was born Sophia Augusta Frederika of Anhalt-Zerbst, a minor league royal of German descent. Plain as a girl, in time, Princess Sophie overcame her pointy chin and long nose with her charm. A palm reader told Sophie that she saw "three crowns in her hand." The girl took the prediction as gospel. "The title of queen fell sweetly on my ear," she wrote in her memoirs. In her mind, she settled on the Grand Duke Peter of Russia. "And gradually, I grew accustomed to thinking that I was destined to be his wife." When the invitation to meet the young Grand Duke arrived, Sophie packed her wedding dress. She became his Grand Duchess Ekaterina (Catherine) Alexeyevna.

"I should have loved my new husband," wrote Catherine in her memoirs, "if only he had been willing or able to be in the least lovable." The teenaged Grand Duke was rude, childish, and nearly a half-wit. He played with toy soldiers in their marital bed and summarily executed rats for breaking "military rules." Eight years in, the passionate Grand Duchess was still a virgin. "I was all but indifferent toward him," she wrote of Peter in her memoirs, "but not so the crown of Russia." She began to find her pleasures among military men. When Peter became Emperor, one of those devoted lovers orchestrated his overthrow. As Empress, Catherine was "the Great," Russia's beloved "Little Mother."

She "has the soul of Brutus," said her buddy, the intellectual Diderot, "combined with the charms of Cleopatra"—or as she put it, "the mind and character of a man with the attractions of a very agreeable woman." By day, with "phenomenal energy," she built schools and hospitals, expanded the Empire to the Baltic, corresponded with intellectuals, and put insurrections to rest. She was heiress to the Russia envisioned by Peter the Great. At night, she became the demanding mistress of the bedroom. Her lovers entered her chamber from a back staircase by a private door. Catherine chose them like a man, demanding fresh young bodies greedily. But no man could be in her company, she bragged, without "feeling at ease."

"My whole existence was devoted to her, much more sincerely than is usually the case when people in such a situation say that," wrote a former lover, whom she made King of Poland to get away from his insistent sheep eyes. She fell hard for the fiery "one-eyed genius," Gregory Potemkin. "My twin-soul," "my golden cock," "my lion of the jungle," she called him, "no man in the world can equal you." Working side-by-side, she bestowed on Potemkin lavish honors and titles, and he may have made Catherine his wife in a secret ceremony. When desire sputtered out, Potemkin became, well, her pimp. In one ruse, he sent a soldier to Catherine with a watercolor to be "studied." She wrote on the back, "the lines are excellent, but the choice of colors is less felicitous."

Who would have refused the all-powerful Empress? Well, no one, of course. Yet the task was considered far from onerous. Even platonic friends like Diderot and Voltaire jealously vied for the stimulating pleasure of the Empress's company. Her sweethearts basked in the glow of her affection, "lost their heads" with love, and preened as the "favorite." When he couldn't get into her room, one lover cried outside the door. Each was like a son—his intellectual progress nurtured, his moods indulged. When *he* wanted to leave, she didn't hold on. She loaded him up with property, and patted him fondly on the tush as he headed out the door.

Catherine's Lesson

Like all Competitor Sirens, Catherine considered sex in league with exercise—a natural form of pleasure and release. It was how she maintained her "physical equilibrium." To ensure that she got what she wanted, she even employed a royal tester. Lovers sometimes struggled to keep up. One ruined his health with aphrodisiacs, which he took to avoid disgrace when he wasn't feeling well. While their "Little Mother" was patient and kind, if "the incident occurred too often, it meant the door."

NEED TO KNOW DEPT.

The Empress not only chose her lovers with an appraiser's eye, but she also made sure there were no unpleasant surprises between the sheets. All candidates were first vetted by Her Majesty's physician. Then an *éprouveuse*, a certain "intrepid" Countess, would subject these lads to the "more intimate test"—a proxy audition. After a detailed report, Catherine weighed the pros and cons and made her final determination. Anything less than the maximum experience wasn't worth her time. She was a busy, busy Empress.

"In politics and love, she was healthy and simple," wrote a biographer. Catherine knew what she wanted and assumed her desires were right and correct. Her voracious libido even demanded the occasional orgy. While many were shocked, those who were close to her rarely were. "One may indulgently close one's eyes to the errors of a woman who is a great man," noted a friend and diplomat. It's been reported that Catherine took only twelve lovers over her lifetime. By today's values, I think we can safely multiply that number by twenty-six.

"The Grand Duchess is romantic, passionate, ardent," said a Chevalier, of young Catherine. "She frightens me." You can't please all of the men, all of the time, but the Siren—particularly the Competitor—doesn't care. She's already mobbed by men who are interested. Mae West, Beryl Markham, the courtesan Ninon de Lenclos—all Competitors—put the pursuit of their pleasure on par with men; and lovers thrilled to the challenge of pleasing them. That mastery and passion, in fact, added sexiness. Decades after their affair, the King of Poland wistfully told Catherine he'd never had it so good. "Now there's a woman for whom a gentleman might take a few blows of knout without regret," said one of her generals.

Key to a Siren's appeal is her sexual vitality. She should have no reservations about looking at him the way he imagines her—in a wet t-shirt, or naked, covered in oil. Maybe sprawled on her bearskin rug, the room lit by the flickering glow of

wood burning in a fireplace, if *Playboy* is our source of inspiration. Or in nothing but waders . . . or is that just me? Royal testers have fallen out of fashion (note to self: business idea?), so you'll have to do your research yourself. Still, you don't need to confuse sex with love and commitment, unless the label fits. If you've dipped your foot into chilly waters, there's no need to submerge.

If it's yours, a raging libido is normal. The Siren who knows who and what she wants in the bedroom is powerful. And power is an aphrodisiac. Don't just "lie back and think of England," as they used to say. Take the initiative and set the pace. Assume responsibility for your pleasure. Tell them how you like it. Give that missionary position a dose of your ecumenical point of view. He may be surprised—at first. But you'll soon find he's more intrigued than ever by you.

walk on the wild side

Angelina Jolie

1975–

Competitor Siren

It's just your average neighborhood barbeque, American style—dogs and burgers hot off the grill. Wives bond over complaints about their husbands. Husbands pop beer cans and trade put-down jokes. Into the fray walks sultry Mary Bell, all cleavage, cheetah print, black leather, and "bee-stung lips." "Who's that?" says Nick, feigning nonchalance, the hairs on his neck rising to the clear and present danger. Why, it's Angelina Jolie, pretty much playing herself—the dark, enigmatic femme fatale. Jolie walked away from the flick *Pushing Tin* with most of the good reviews and her co-star. It wouldn't be the last time. "I left our home to work on a movie, and while I was away my boyfriend got married," said actress Laura Dern, blindsided. Angelina wore Billy Bob Thornton's blood in a vial around her neck and was having such athletic sex she said there was no need for a gym. Gulp.

You can probably count on your pinky finger the number of women you know who, in the throes of depression, have hired a hit man to take them out (the hit man talked Jolie out of it). Or who have considered a career as a funeral director. While I myself have never dreamt of tying the knot in "a small black wedding" (first marriage, to Jonny Lee Miller), I try to imagine circumstances in which I might warm to the inscription "Till the End" in blood over my nuptial bed (Billy Bob). There is, by the way, a reasonable explanation for Jolie's fascination with knives. Young Angie's late mother took her to Renaissance fairs, which feature medieval weaponry. Yet, she takes an interest in the most *curious* details. Inspecting weapons on the set of the action film *Mr. and Mrs. Smith*, in which she plays a housewife-cum-assassin, Jolie wondered, "Does this come with a serrated

lead them to the bedroom **181**

blade? And which particular kind of hook, once you stick it into somebody, is good for ripping their flesh on the way out?" Ahem.

"Honestly, I like everything. Boyish girls, girlish boys, the heavy and the skinny. Which is a problem when I'm walking down the street."

—*Angelina Jolie*

It may bear repeating that Angelina Jolie is the daughter of actor Jon Voight and the late actress Marcheline Bertrand. In kindergarten, Angelina and her precocious pals formed The Kissy Girls. "We would chase the boys around and kiss them a lot, and they would scream," she explained. Was this the beginning of it all? Adolescence brought early storm warnings. Girly dress-up was traded for dog collars and studs, and a boyfriend with whom she exchanged near-lethal knife wounds.

"Looking back, he was somebody that I wanted to help me break out," she said. Mercy, girl, don't we all know exactly how *that* feels? Suicide, Jolie realized, was "a door I can walk through anytime," so she decided to "live hard and not give a shit." The movie *Girl, Interrupted* showed just how far she'd step out on that limb. The director cast her as a seductive sociopath for that aura of danger she projects—a "Jack Nicholson in drag," were his words. "I lived completely on impulse," she said of playing the role. She likes to shock, said a director, to "be that person in the room who's willing to put it out there." *Movieline* voted Jolie "most likely to scare a psychiatrist."

Jolie has fashioned a persona as a sex adventuress, and motherhood hasn't tempered it. Let's review the history: she has extolled the joys of S & M, talked of hooking up with faceless lovers in hotel rooms, and plunged into a much-publicized affair with a woman. "Honestly, I like everything," she said in an interview, "Boyish girls, girlish boys." For a while, it looked like that might even include siblings. "You're the most amazing man I've ever known, and I love you," she said, grabbing her Oscar and giving her brother a soulful smooch on the lips. Then came the *coup de grâce*: she stole the world's sexiest man away from his wife, the fantasy girl next door. Now we're not even sure what she intends to do with him.

"She wants to make all men kneel at her feet," says a friend. And like all Competitor Sirens, Jolie rises best to the challenge of the man who's otherwise engaged. Her Siren song is her passionate fearlessness. He's awestruck by the woman who's sometimes more of a man than he is himself. "I mean, he really *is* a homemaker," said Doug Liman, the director of *Mr. and Mrs. Smith*. "But for Angie, bringing her into that suburban home . . . I might as well have asked her to simulate being on a spacecraft." The thrill is in the chase of keeping up with her—especially in the bedroom. The notable softening since Jolie has become a mother and Goodwill Ambassador for the U.N.? The Competitor will always trade hearth and home for the sexual challenge.

Angelina's Lesson

Gather a group of avowedly heterosexual men in a room, and ask them who is the sexiest woman dominating the tabloids. You'll get Catherine Zeta-Jones, Scarlett Johansson, and Halle Berry, for sure—maybe a wildcard, like Sarah Jessica Parker. But the vote won't be unanimous until the name Angelina Jolie comes up, which is also when the temperature in the room starts to rise.

It's the luscious lips, the pan-ethnic beauty, the body that trumped even the computer-generated Lara Croft when Angelina brought *Tomb Raider* to the screen. She holds the distinction, in fact, of being the "Sexiest Woman Alive" many times over in magazines around the world. What thrills men to the depths of their souls is not the undeniable beauty, though it doesn't hurt. It's that Angelina Jolie is more than a little dangerous. "She has no limits . . . it feels like she'll try anything," is what they say. In fact, she prides herself on how far she'll go.

For a scene in *Mr. and Mrs. Smith*, the director suggested Jolie perform the "most graphic, crazy sex act I could imagine, ten steps beyond anything I'd consider," just to see her reaction. When Jolie furrowed her brow, he thought he'd finally succeeded in shocking her. "No, actually," she said, cool as the proverbial cucumber, "I'm just trying to figure out whether I've *done* that one."

Jolie has "A prayer for the wild at heart kept in cages"—a quote from Tennessee Williams, which is also tattooed across her forearm. That's not an accident. She has repeatedly claimed that when it comes to sex, she likes "everything." Until Jolie installs a camera in her bedroom, we won't be privy to what that means. But you just *know* that she's entered territory where the lights and running water don't work. Asked if she prefers danger or sex, she said, "there is no sex without danger." She walks on the wild side. There's no telling what she'll do.

Are vials of blood really necessary? Must one collect a full complement of whips and leather? How exactly do knives figure in the erotic tableau? Does somebody really have to get hurt? Hey, don't ask me, I caved when my niece asked me where babies come from. But if we've learned anything from Angelina Jolie, it's that opening the door to your darker fantasies is a definite turn-on. It might give you exactly the kind of Siren reputation you need.

Does he dream of making love in places where you're bound to get caught? Do you? My advice: don't knock sex on car tops, in sand traps, or in the deep end of swimming pools until you've tried it once or twice. I'm no Angie, but here's my story: on vacation in Maine, my boyfriend and I snuck into the house of volunteer firemen for an erotic interlude while they were responding to a call. We left a note thanking our hosts for the 600-thread count. Years later, my old boyfriend still brings it up. The situation gave him an erotic charge.

Is it time to simulate that hostage situation? The dominatrix role? The virgin sacrifice? Jump in with enthusiasm. Offer to tape it for the Internet—look what it did for that Hilton girl. If Bree from *Desperate Housewives* can loosen her apron for a little S & M, it might be time for you to try something dangerous. Every man wants a bad girl in the bedroom. Why not you?

talk dirty

Mae West

(née Mary Jane West)

1892–1980

Competitor/Goddess Siren

As the platinum-blonde singer Flower Belle Lee, Mae West saunters into Greasewood City, a lawless town in the Wild West on a back lot in Hollywood. In the flick *My Little Chickadee*, West is as shapely as a mountain range and as steamy as high noon, a woman designed to stir up desire and trouble in every scene she steals. Taking over for Greasewood's wilting schoolmarm, Flower Belle brings a roomful of unruly boys to attention—provoking the inevitable bug eyes and cat calls. "I always *was* good at figgers," she drawls, meaning arithmetic, but with a knowing drift to her voice that implies something more. "One and one makes two, two and two makes four, and five makes ten if you work it right."

"It's not what I do, but how I do it. It isn't what I say, but how I say it, and how I look when I do and say it," explained Mae West. On paper, lines like, "Come up, and see me sometime," or "Beulah, peel me a grape," were perfectly innocent. West took "Victorian care," in fact, with her word choice. But that languorous delivery flashed Sex! Sex! Sex! as insistently as a neon sign over a Dutch bordello. "Goodness, what beautiful diamonds!" says *I'm No Angel*'s hat check girl. "Goodness had nothin' to do with it, dearie," drawls West, her voice dripping with innuendo.

From her earliest reckoning, Mary Jane West was steered by her mother toward a career in vaudeville. At seven years old, she found performing erotic, or as she put it, "like the strongest man's arms around me, like an ermine coat." Her songs were risqué, whetting her appetite for the aroused male. She favored tough guys—boxers, bodyguards, shady lawyers—and the intrigue of juggling boyfriends. Her mother told her that marriage was a swift ticket to nowhere. Fidelity was not for her anyway, Mae owned. Yet for mysterious reasons, at nineteen, she married a song-and-dance man named Frank Wallace on the sly, and then packed her bags and hit the road. Three decades later, Wallace blew her cover when he sued for divorce.

NEED TO KNOW DEPT.

By her own account, Mae West first experienced an orgasm during a dream featuring a large furry bear who "entered her bedroom and then her body." Thereafter she was apparently calibrated to climax in thirty seconds.

Mae's big break was the Broadway revue *A La Broadway and Hello Paris.* When audiences clamored for encores, West gave them seven, stunning producers with lyrics she'd written herself. It was the beginning of her long campaign of shock and awe. "I only knew two rules of playwriting," she claimed. "Write about what you know, and make it entertaining." Her play *Sex* opened in 1926 in New London, moved to Broadway, and stirred the Society for the Suppression of Vice into high gear. Mae was thrown into jail, resulting in reams of valuable publicity. In 1928, the whole cast of *The Pleasure Man* was hauled off. With *Diamond Lil*, West hit on the character that would become her trademark. Lil was a souped up version of West herself—a voluptuous, campy, man-eating broad, who did what she wanted and was beholden to no one.

Diamond Lil came to the Hollywood screen as *She Done Him Wrong.* Spotting a young unknown Cary Grant on the Paramount lot, Mae said, "If he can talk, I'll take him." Grant was cast as a young undercover cop, corrupted by Lady Lou, Mae's now forty-year-old nightclub chanteuse. What Lou lost in dialogue cut by the censors was picked up in West's delivery. "Why don't you come up and see me sometime," was an invitation whose implication audiences didn't mistake. It was all in the impudent jut of her hip, the drawl, and the appraising way she looked at a man. West's comic vulgarity was a box office smash. By 1934, her movies had pulled Paramount back from the brink of ruin.

PHONE IT IN

Once you've got talking dirty down, take it to the phone lines—or e-mail. You don't have to "go all the way" *every* time. Tell him what you'd like to do as soon as you get your hands all over him.

What Mae West brought to the pictures was an astonishing personality, which carried over into real life. She was a masculine mind in the most feminine body in Hollywood—the Competitor Siren's blueprint. In her view, women depended too much on one man for happiness. She took lovers the way others ordered pizza. Mae seized pleasure where she found it, not needing love for its justification. She didn't smoke, drink, or swear, and attended Sunday Mass to save her soul. And yet dirty talk was her hallmark. She's still considered one of the sexiest dames, living or dead, in Hollywood.

At seventy-seven, West made a comeback as a modern-day Diamond Lil in the movie *Myra Breckinridge*. She played Leticia Van Allen, a Hollywood agent with an active casting couch. At age eighty-five, in the movie *Sextette*, she fended off discarded ex-husbands Timothy Dalton and George Hamilton, who were young enough to be her grandsons. By then, I'll admit, she looked embalmed. She died in the arms of her lover Paul Novak, an actor/bodybuilder half her age, who claimed he'd been "put on this earth to take care of Mae West."

Mae's Lesson

"Mae West couldn't sing a lullaby without making it sexy," wrote *Variety*. She could also take a bawdy line and make it sound angelic, simply by clasping her hands next to her cheek and looking heavenward. "I speak two languages," she explained, "English and Body"—always simultaneously. To sex up a line, she relied on double entendre and manipulated her "voice and figure like an accomplished musician with an instrument." With that slow drawl, deft timing, and a body that appeared to be in perpetual motion even when she was standing still, West suggested volumes without actually saying anything specific. She confounded the censors, who combed her lines. "Haven't you ever found a man to make you happy?" asks Cary Grant. "Sure," says Lou, pause, voluptuous glance, "lots of times." It's not the words, but, as she said, the "sex personality" that makes it work.

Without ever uttering a salacious word, Mae West managed to show us all the erotic power of dirty talk. In *Bartlett's Familiar Quotations*, you'll find some of West's most popular lines, still imitated in her sultry delivery. If you can summon the idea of sex in his mind while you're reciting the Lord's Prayer, you don't need Mae's help. Not sex in the abstract—he's doing that every ten seconds anyway (or so say the experts). I mean the fantasy of *you* straddled over his steaming Harley—or whatever works. If not, let Mae show you how.

Cock your hip. Offer up some of your insolence. Then, say it slow, like a purr. Give every syllable meaningful emphasis, as if you want to jump his bones (because, of course, you do). A three-syllable word becomes four—that is, when you drawl. If you time it right, the whole thing could take all morning, particularly if he acts on your suggestive tone.

Unlike Mae, you are not restrained by censorship. Actually, neither was she—in the bedroom. It's time to kick it up a notch. If you're wary, summon up the courage. After all, you're a fearless Siren. Talk dirty in the bedroom, using all the explicit details. Need something to break the ice first? MyPleasure.com recommends reading aloud from *The Erotic Edge* or *Delta of Venus*—new to me, but perhaps not to Amazon. Once you've weaned yourself on the written word, come up with your own descriptions. Tell him what you're going to do to him, step-by-step, and then do it. His anticipation is the key. Switch it up, and imagine out loud what he might do to you in return. Throw in a *soupçon* of sexually explicit profanity.

It's not so much what you say but how you say it, men claim—which sounds like Mae's advice. Describing an erotic act can sound as clinical as *The Kinsey Report*, if you do it wrong. Breathe slow and deep through parted lips. A few Kittenish sounds of pleasure wouldn't hurt. Put a little catch in your throat on the exhale. Hey, I'm not making this up, I'm getting it from SexInfo101.com. Don't rehearse, lest you sound like a porn film. And don't use words of love. Aim for the anonymous.

MORE MAE

Is that a gun in your pocket, or are you just glad to see me?

I used to be Snow White, but I drifted.

It's not the men in your life, it's the life in your men.

So many men, so little time.

Anything worth doing is worth doing slowly.

Give a man a free hand and he'll run it all over you.

I've been in more laps than a napkin.

I generally avoid temptation unless I can't resist it.

*When choosing between two evils, I always like to take
the one I've never tried before.*

All discarded lovers should be given a second chance, but with somebody else.

When women go wrong, men go right after them.

switch hit

Colette

(née Sidonie-Gabrielle Colette)

1873–1954

Competitor/Sex Kitten Siren

"As if the first caress had wounded her, she . . . turned a marvelous, animal face toward me," wrote Colette in the steamy classic *Claudine Married*, published in 1901. What a bodice ripper! "Everything melted into wild surrender, into murmuring, imperious demands, into a kind of amorous fury, followed by childish 'Thank-yous' and great, satisfied sighs of 'Ah!' like a little girl who had been dreadfully thirsty. . . ." Claudine on her wedding night? Not quite. Stepping out on her husband, Renaud? Yes, but with a piquant twist. The scene is a rendezvous between Claudine and her gal pal Rézi—an affair enthusiastically endorsed by Renaud from the sidelines. In sales, the novel topped Colette's *Claudine at School*, which had spawned a rash of boyish Claudine look-alikes in Parisian brothels. As readers of *Claudine Married* would learn, Renaud was *also* sleeping with Rézi behind Claudine's back.

Colette channeled her life into her work almost as fast as she lived it. And in her much-publicized marriage to the journalist known as Willy, it was no secret that "Rézi" was their shared mistress. "Colette has claimed the high ground . . . in this murky tale," wrote Henri Gauthier-Villars (Willy) in his memoirs. "Bull! Bull! In reality, it was she—seduced from the moment they met—who courted [my mistress]." And Willy was endlessly titillated by the arrangement. Turning her life into art, Colette tapped into the French psyche; her character's greedy sexuality struck a chord. In the Belle Epoque, were respectable women supposed to know quite so much about what turned men on?

Born in a small village in Burgundy, Sidonie-Gabrielle Colette married Willy—an older friend of the family—while she was still in braids and a sailor suit. He lent his name to ghost-written novels, which he tricked up with salacious details and then sold. It wasn't long before he pressed Colette into earning her keep. He judged her first effort, *Claudine at School*, "commercially worthless." It languished in a drawer for two years. On rediscovering the manuscript, Willy was strangely aroused by Claudine's crush on Aimée, her pretty assistant school mistress. Willy locked Colette in a room to write and told her to "warm it up." The Claudine novels—bestsellers all—came out under his name, until she left Willy and struck out on her own. The young, Kittenish Colette traded her magnificent braids for cropped hair and cat-eyes lined with kohl—and the frank sexuality of a Competitor Siren.

"If I can't have too many truffles, I'll do without truffles."

—Colette

"So many women want to be corrupted, and so few are chosen!" wrote Colette in the homoerotic *The Pure and the Impure*. Colette's books introduced something new: a woman who not only overtly desired, but did so within gender lines. In life and art, Colette hopped from male to female lover and back again. On the Moulin Rouge stage, she went just a bit too far. In an exotic pantomime called *Rêve d'Égypte*, written by Willy, Colette appeared as a gilded mummy. Her real-life lover, Missy, played an archaeologist who seductively unwrapped and kissed her. "Down with the dykes!" shouted the crowd, who pelted them with orange peels and seat cushions—and bought tickets for her next show.

In her novels, Colette captured the old turn-of-the-century "Paris of refinement," but with rapturous new revelations of its secrets of the flesh. Her novels were "just dirty enough—and the dirt was just arty enough" to be taken seriously.

She wracked up literary awards. Colette "eagerly picked the fruits of the earth" without morality judgments. Words like, "Vice is doing wrong without enjoying it," came out of the mouths of babes like Claudine. Colette lived by it.

When Colette took up with Bertrand de Jouvenal, the son of her estranged second husband, Henri, she in effect added incest to her quiver. "My primary impression was of power, and a power whose shock was sweet to me," said young Bertrand, of their five-year affair. "The pleasure she gave . . . opened a window on the world." Domination, submission, open marriage, orgasm, infidelity, rape, bondage, and sadism—in essays and novels, she covered it all. In the panorama of sexual behavior, could you ask for anything more? Yet, it was Colette's open bisexuality—in life and in print—that sealed her reputation as a sensualist.

In addition to classic novels such as *The Vagabond*, *The Shackle*, and *Chéri*, Colette wrote memoirs, essays, stories, stage plays, and, notably, the book that was the basis for the delicious movie *Gigi*. Her third marriage, to a jewel merchant sixteen years her junior, was the one that took. Before they even met, he decided to marry Colette after reading her books. "What binds me to Maurice and him to me?" she mused. "It's my virility."

As the French say, *chacun à son goût*.

Colette's Lesson

In a radio interview, Colette pondered the insatiable sexual habits of Don Juan. Her take? Men are wildly envious of the sexual pleasure women experience. In their need for conquest, they are trying to reach that bliss themselves. It could explain their fixation on that girl-on-girl thing, so graphically illustrated in videos and photos that make the rounds on the Internet. Remember when it seemed that actress Anne Heche's stay on the Isle of Lesbos would doom her career? Little did we know it would be a rallying point. How about Angelina Jolie's admission, "I like everything—boyish girls, girlish boys"? It made her dangerous, for sure, but also infinitely more thrilling. That footage of Madonna kissing Britney still has a life of its own, and that's because the switch hit is a home run.

SPILL THE BEANS

"I'm a lesbian. What do you do?" said actress Tallulah Bankhead, introducing herself at a party. In the long list of laugh lines she delivered, this was the hands-down favorite. A much-publicized affair with actress Eva Le Gallienne, among others, established Bankhead as a flashy switch hitter. Whiskey-voiced, outrageous, irresistible, Bankhead knew it never hurts a Siren to reveal she takes it as far as it goes.

While my personal experience in this realm is woefully limited, I've seen that a Siren's reputation never suffers when she steps out on a limb—particularly with another beautiful woman. At the summer theater where I worked years ago, no one got more play than a girlish assistant director, who was fresh off an affair with a woman. Maybe that's just what she said to turn men on. Whatever. It worked. They spent their waking hours imagining it and her.

"Nobody fantasizes about things they don't like," writes Bob Berkowitz in *His Secret Self*. What men fantasize about most is the *ménage à trois*—two women per man for double the fun. The arrangement has the seal of approval from the *Kamasutra*, which says group sex is always better when she enlists her buds. This is often how men conjure it up. The fantasy begins innocently—say, over dinner with the wife and her friend. Soon, the wine is flowing freely, the clothes are off, and he gets to watch. As Renaud tells Claudine, cheating is "a matter of gender." For him, an affair between women doesn't count. It's just for fun.

So, now you know.

If you're currently or have ever been a switch hitter, don't keep it to yourself. Offer up those naughty bits he longs to hear. If it doesn't scare him to death—and it might—you'll be more darkly alluring. Maybe, just maybe, you're on the brink. You need Colette's liberated prose to spur you on. As they say, you go for it girl. You can always put that gooey chocolate back in the box if it isn't for you. Wait, are those beads of sweat collecting on your brow? Relax. Colette wouldn't have you do what doesn't turn you on, although I suspect she'd think you're hopelessly bourgeois.

"You will do foolish things, but do them with enthusiasm."

— *Colette*

Bring in a recruit, or just say you will. The fantasy can be as effective as the reality—for most men, more so. A man with "'Hot Lesbian Auditions!'" on his mind doesn't necessarily want to open the show. He just wants you to take the stage in his mind.

ARE YOU LEADING THEM TO THE BEDROOM?

You have enormous sex appeal, of course, but are you leading them to the bedroom? Are you a woman of your word or full of sexual promises you fail to keep? Say "yes" more often than not, and you're a Siren who makes them salivate.

✦ Are you conscious of setting the erotic stage, even while you go about your everyday activities?

✦ Have you been called a "bad girl"?

✦ In a conversation with a man, are you as aware of the way you say something as you are of what you say?

✦ Do you avoid sexual routine?

✦ Are you willing to act on a man's fantasies, even when they seem over the top?

✦ Are you unembarrassed to discuss or play out your own fantasies?

✦ Do you feel that a woman's sexual satisfaction is as important as a man's?

✦ Do you like sex that is dangerous in some way?

✦ Have you ever fantasized about making love to another woman?

✦ Does talking about sex turn you on?

✦ Do some kinds of pornography give you an erotic charge?

✦ Do you feel there are times when it's important for a woman to take the sexual initiative?

Think More Like a Man

(in Matters of the Heart)

"Why can't a woman be more like a man?" wondered Henry Higgins in *My Fair Lady*. The Siren who *thinks* like a man is unstoppable. Double standards have no meaning, simply because she pays no attention to them. She takes her romantic destiny in her own hands—adding voltage to her magnetism. She's a Siren who knows who she is and what she wants, and isn't afraid to go after it. What's more, she's big enough to accept the consequences.

What does it mean to think like a man in matters of the heart? It depends on the Siren you talk to. To one it's an independence of spirit, to another it's playing the field. But just because a Siren thinks like a man doesn't mean she abandons her awesome femininity. In the seventeenth century, the courtesan Ninon de Lenclos pledged to live like a man—and did—without burning her corset. More than four centuries later, feminists marvel at her Siren power and her extraordinary presence in French society. Ninon's lessons are as true today as they were in the Renaissance. The same may be said of England's Siren Queen, Elizabeth I. In the sixteenth century, her refusal to commit was part of her charm. During the Jazz Age, Zelda Sayre kept her edge by playing the field. Decades later, Camilla Parker-Bowles, always the aggressor, wrote her own script and played it out as she dreamed.

To think more like a man, allow these Sirens to lead the way. These bold seductresses put you in the driver's seat.

refuse to commit

Queen Elizabeth 1 of England

1533–1603

Goddess/Competitor Siren

Long ago, in a kingdom far away, lived a queen who couldn't decide which man to marry: the King of Spain, a Duke from France, or one of a phalanx of titled noblemen. For decades, in fact, Queen Elizabeth kept her court in suspense, and they had long given up on wedding plans. The "Virgin Queen" would die without an heir, potentially throwing her kingdom into civil war. But in her forty-sixth year, hope loomed on the horizon in the twenty-two-year-old Duc de Alençon, the younger brother of the King of France. An ambassador stepped ashore to negotiate the union for the "bandy-legged" duke, whom the Queen called "my very dear frog" in love notes. Bess was playing for keeps this time. This was her last hope of continuing her dynasty. She pranced, she flirted, she affectionately called the French ambassador her "monkey," all while her advisors squirmed in their seats with embarrassment. Swept away by her charm, the ambassador reported back that the "bonny" Queen was irresistible. By the time the duke crossed the channel to press his suit, the courtship had reached a fevered pitch. The "lovers" all but fell into each other's arms. But . . . but . . . in the final hour, Elizabeth couldn't quite bring herself to sign the contract. The Queen was, well, a commitment-phobe.

Elizabeth I was the daughter of the infamous Anne Boleyn and King Henry VIII, one of the most catastrophic couplings in history. After Anne gave birth to Elizabeth instead of a boy, the King had her beheaded on trumped up charges of adultery. Things didn't go smoothly for Princess Bess, especially after King Henry passed on. She was imprisoned in the Tower of London by Queen Mary I, her half

sister, who feared Bess's threat to her throne—Mary didn't come by the nickname "Bloody Mary" for nothing. Bess dodged execution by seeming to favor no particular religion, party, or point of view. Indecision was her camouflage.

"My Lords, do whatever you wish. As for me, I shall do no otherwise than pleases me."

—Elizabeth I

By all accounts, red-haired Elizabeth was a dead ringer for her dad, more "comely" than beautiful. At ten years old, she amused Henry "with wise and witty conversation," as if she were a woman of twenty-five. Her precocious charm enchanted everyone. Men were bowled over by Elizabeth's lightning mind, described as "without womanly weakness" by her tutor. Always dressed in dazzling splendor, she combined majesty with the common touch, intimacy with

distance, and gravity with wit—ever the vibrant and elusive paradox. "Her eye was set upon one, her ear listed to another, her judgment ran upon a third, to a fourth she addressed her speech; her spirit seemed to be everywhere. . . ." She formed "quasi-erotic" relationships with her advisors and easily inspired their loyalty. From the moment Bess was crowned at twenty-five, they obsessed over whom she would take to bed.

Philip II of Spain, Thomas Seymour, Archduke Ferdinand of Austria and his brother Charles, Prince Eric of Sweden, and Sir William Pickering came a calling—and all were frustrated. The Goddess set the terms in the first year of her reign. "I have already joined myself in marriage to a Husband, namely, the Kingdom England," she told her Parliament. But no one believed that she meant what she said. Flashing the matrimonial card, she played France against Spain, the two superpowers of the day. Elizabeth hinted to France's Henri II that she would break off marriage talk with King Philip of Spain—if he would just do her a teensy weensy favor and give her back Calais. She left Philip endlessly dangling to keep Spain on her side. In the end, Elizabeth usually got what she wanted, and her suitors were stonewalled. This was before news traveled at the speed of sound.

"Virgin or not?" everyone speculated. Few disputed her abiding passion for Robert Dudley, the Earl of Leicester—the pal who shared the hopes and fears of her terrorized childhood. When he pressed too hard for marriage, she famously said, "I will have here but one mistress and no master." Dudley married twice, but rarely left Bess's side. "You are like my little dog," she noted, perhaps not very flatteringly. "When people see you, they know I am nearby." By denying them what they wanted but urging them on, Elizabeth kept them coming back for more—which is exactly the way she liked it.

Elizabeth's most sensational act was beheading her cousin Mary, Queen of Scots, the beautiful fool who plotted her downfall. But she was one of the most dazzling monarchs in English history. When she acted, she acted decisively. She rallied England against the Spanish Armada and defeated them. Her encouragement of artists such as Shakespeare led England into a golden cultural age. She set her country on the road to the great empire it would become. She went to her grave after forty-four years as queen, just as she foresaw—uncommitted and virginal. Her cousin James, Mary's son, followed her on the throne.

Bess's Lesson

Elizabeth's father, King Henry VIII, bullied all six of his wives and sent two to the scaffold. Elizabeth's half sister, Mary I, tussled with her husband, Philip of Spain, over who would wear the royal pants. Two of her stepmothers died in agonized childbirth. In short, Elizabeth saw just how "dangerous love could be." At nine years old, she swore to Robert Dudley that she would never marry. As Queen, marriage became incompatible to her ruling shtick. She saw she could use her refusal to commit to get what she needed—and more.

LOVE THE ONE YOU'RE WITH

Elizabeth was "tirelessly fond" of her suitors. It's one of the reasons she was able to keep them hopefully dangling for years and years. Each suitor seemed to shake to the core her conviction to "live and die a Virgin." Like all Sirens, Bess loved men—but particularly the one standing right in front of her. Each believed he was "The One," especially because Elizabeth seemed to think so herself. She fell head over heels in love, only to fall out of love when the idea of commitment became real. Love the one you're with—heart, body, and soul—even if it's just for today. They'll love you more for adoring them.

"She has many suitors for her hand," noted the Venetian Ambassador, "and by protracting any decision keeps them all in hope, persuading herself that in her need they will do what they can from rivalry to gain her love and matrimonial alliance." The "mistress of equivocation" delighted in baiting her poor suitors and in outraging her court. All women naturally want to marry, they thought. In time, Elizabeth would cave in. But she never let their expectations set her course. The result? The image of her power and charm became "almost mythological."

Was Elizabeth's sixteenth-century situation so out of sync with the expectations of today? Don't men always assume women want commitment? And don't they often feel the need to elude it for as long as they can? As soon as *you* want it casual, they want more—that is, if they believe you at all. Elizabeth's lesson is common sense. The balance of power always rests with the party who's willing to walk away. Men sometimes get sloppy on the slam-dunk. They're on their best behavior when they're in negotiating mode.

Here's a chapter in my romantic history worth offering up, though I'll admit it doesn't reflect particularly well on me: I dated a best-selling novelist for a while—not for himself, but for the love of the glamorous life he led. I told him the truth: I'm in this for fun. He thought this was my crafty way of pretending to be unattainable. For years, I mean years, after it was over, he kept coming around. He finally admitted that my power over him was especially potent because I'd never entirely succumbed. He got his revenge. He based a character in a novel on me—a biatch who meets her end in a gruesome accident. I don't know, I like to think that I was immortalized.

When a man is confronted with a dame who pushes away, reverse psychology kicks in. "I can't live without her," he thinks, forgetting that he probably will. Advance, retreat, hold your cards close to your chest. Then put them back down on the table again. Instead of chasing the end game of marriage, take a page from the playbook of Elizabeth I. Banish those images of that fluffy white dress from your head. Don't practice taking his name as yours. Make flirtation your "life blood." Enjoy them all in the moment, but be unsure of where it will go. He'll be crazy with love.

Elizabeth never tired of the game because it suited her purposes. But maybe commitment and marriage *is* what you want. Still, there's a deeper lesson to be learned. Companion, Competitor, or Goddess, the wise Siren never gives up all of herself. In the words of my friend Hope, "she has a soap opera she can call her own" and an independence of spirit that is untouchable. Self-determination is way sexy. The less you are in need of him, the more irresistible you'll be.

go after what you want
and damn the consequences

CASE STUDY:
Camilla Shand Parker-Bowles

1947–

Competitor/Mother Siren

On a rain-soaked afternoon in 1972, Camilla Shand waltzed up to Charles, the Prince of Wales, on the Windsor polo fields. "My great-grandmother was your great-great-grandfather's mistress," she said. "How about it?" In the movie version—had there been one—Camilla would have been dressed like a fashion plate, all creamy cashmere and Gucci accessories. But, no, in reality she wore muddy Wellington boots, her frowzy cords, and an old green jacket. The humidity played havoc with her bad haircut. Yet, Charles's attraction to Camilla was instant. She was armed with her confidence, always formidable, and a sense of personal destiny. Within weeks she had captured the heart of the Prince of Wales—for good. Yet, she turned down his proposal. Her past was already too steamy to aim for Queen.

The great-great-grandfather of this story, King Edward VII, had many, many mistresses—a few of whom populate the pages of *Simply Irresistible*. But Alice Keppel was acknowledged as "La Favorita." Edward had mistresses more flashy and beautiful, but Alice soothed his royal soul. "Her charm was not in her looks," wrote a biographer. In fact, her husband, George, was the pretty one. Alice was good fun when Edward was bored. She was patient with his tempers and endlessly sympathetic to his needs. "Like all successful mistresses," wrote an observer, "she was part lover, part wife, part mother." With Alice, Edward was comfortable. Camilla was more than ready to assume the role—though she came in a flavor a little more "devil-may-care" and earthy. Even in school, Camilla Shand had a

"magnetism," reported a classmate. "She didn't need to be anything other than she was." And what she was, was a sexy Competitor Siren. Confident, spirited, bawdy, she was far more popular as a London debutante than prettier girls, even while she favored "unhip twin sets and tweed skirts." "Milla" was never shy or tongue-tied. She always had something amusing to say. Men admired her ruthlessness on the foxhunting field. "Get out of the fucking way!" was her bugle call—which applied in love as well. Setting her sights on the rakish Andrew Parker-Bowles, she literally marked him as hers. Years into her marriage to Parker-Bowles, she resumed where she had left off—as La Favorita of Charles.

"There are three of us in this marriage," said Princess Diana, the virgin bride Camilla had handpicked. Oh, you don't think so? The absolute proof had come out in "Camillagate." In an intimate telephone conversation that was taped by a reporter, Charles dreamed of being reincarnated as Camilla's Tampax—for reasons too obvious to bother mentioning here. The truth broke like a levee in a level five hurricane. Charles and Camilla led, in effect, double lives in an eighteenth-century manor house they called their own. They threw dinner parties and traveled secretly together on holiday. She organized his life, offered advice, and listened to the woes of the beleaguered prince. The public didn't understand. How could Charles prefer the doughty Camilla to his exquisite Princess?

"PRINCE CHARLES SEVERS ALL LINKS WITH CAMILLA PARKER-BOWLES: MY DUTY BEFORE LOVE," trumpeted a London headline. Dream on. They underestimated the staying power of a Mother Siren with a game plan. Camilla fixed herself a stiff drink and fielded volumes of hate mail. The lovers laid low. In Camilla, the Prince had a safe haven. She apparently had him in "sexual thrall." Princess Diana didn't have a prayer. Sure, Diana had mastered style, celebrity, even a kind of sainthood. But the art of being a Siren had eluded her. Diana left Charles, and not long after, she was killed in a car crash. As far as the world was concerned, Camilla now had blood on her hands.

Thirty-three years after that day on the polo fields, Charles proposed to Camilla for the second time. The ring was an eight-carat heirloom, and she reported "just coming down to earth" from the heavenly thrill of it all. But England didn't easily forgive and forget. It would never do to have Camilla on the throne. She was dubbed the Princess Consort and the Duchess of Cornwall—all things considered, not bad for a commoner. But wasn't living the secret life of La Favorita way more fun?

MASTER THE PICK-UP LINE

You shoved three women out of the way, and now you're standing right in front of him. Alas, your great grandmother wasn't Alice Keppel, nor is he the Prince of Wales—so you don't have the perfect opener prepared. Those lame pick-up lines that men get busted for? They can be quite charming on the woman who uses them with irony. Why not, "what's a nice boy like you doing in a place like this?" You could even invite him to your studio to peruse your etchings. Throw down the sexual gauntlet with a line that's a bit of a tease: "The bride says we'd make beautiful music together," you say to the best man. "Tell me a little more about your instrument."

Camilla's Lesson

"She would have the life she wanted—she exuded that," reported one of her classmates. And the life she wanted included the Prince of Wales. The family history ordained it. "She was always mentioning it," reported one of her early beaus, "as if it were something almost talismanic." In a symbolic gesture, she even took the middle name "Rosemary"—after Alice Keppel's daughter by King Edward VII. "Your greatest achievement is to love me," said Prince Charles on the Camillagate tapes. This was a point she did not dispute.

Would Camilla have fallen in love with Charles were he not a Prince? Who can say, and does it really matter at this point? Her devotion is clearly genuine. What their contemporaries found more intriguing still was why Charles even noticed Camilla in such a crowded field. "There were all kinds of glamorous women around," said an observer—and, like Camilla, any number were throwing themselves at him. By some accounts, she researched her prey. She figured out what Charles needed most and laid it on. She became the first person in his "loveless life who truly understood him, who answered his needs, and who listened to his thoughts." That mix of Mother Siren and brazen Competitor Siren was a complete turn-on to him.

History is chock full of Sirens who went after what they wanted—from Cleopatra to the Duchess of Windsor (to whom Camilla is eerily parallel). A seductress with a sense of destiny is hard to stop, particularly when she relies on her confidence. The man on the receiving end is more flattered than he might at first be willing to admit—a fact that my friend Sabina confirms. She literally spied her first husband from across a crowded art gallery floor. Instead of contriving a way to be introduced, she caught his eye and beckoned. Sabina's always had balls, and a strong sense of her curb appeal. By the end of the evening, Steve was sitting in *her* lap at a bar downtown. Sabina's moved on. That was years ago. But she's always gotten what she wanted by putting herself right in front of him.

"I really need a gin and tonic."

—*Camilla Parker-Bowles, after meeting Charles's sons*

Here's the rub: when you go after what you want, it doesn't necessarily make you popular. No one knows this better than the Duchess of Cornwall. As Diana was deified, Camilla was blackballed. She's been savaged in the press. The Princess privately called Camilla "the rottweiler" and leaked this to the tabloids. A lesser woman might not have been able to withstand the constant scrutiny. You know what? Camilla carried on. "Never explain, never complain," has always been her credo.

See a man you fancy from across the room? Part the crowds to get to him. Decide that whatever you want, you'll get that—and more. Hearts are moved by a woman with purpose, as long as she employs her Siren skills. Your resolve itself is part of the juggernaut that hurtles you toward success in your goals. Let the proverbial chips fall where they might. Go for what you want, and damn the consequences.

call your own shots

Ninon de Lenclos

1620–1705

Companion/Competitor Siren

"You will forget and betray me. I know your heart, it alarms me, crushes me," complained the Marquis de la Châtre, before departing on an extended trip. "Now, I wish you to put in writing that you will remain faithful to me. . . ." Always tender toward her lovers, Ninon de Lenclos gently argued that such a pledge would be foolish. Yet, what's a lady to do? She could not bear to keep the Marquis in anguished suspense. She gave him her written vow—which she promptly broke within two days. *Billet de la Châtre*, in fact, came to mean a contract not worth the paper it was written on.

Ninon de Lenclos lived by her own laws, often distinctly at odds with the code of the day. This was doubly so in her love relationships. She "regarded desire as a purely blind, mechanical or chemical force." Since romantic love was fleeting, fidelity was ludicrous. Sounds vaguely twentieth century, doesn't it? While other women irritated with their peccadilloes, Ninon was unfaithful with "such judgment" it was felt that a man "did himself an injury to blame her."

Born without property in Renaissance France—akin to being a nobody—young Anne de Lenclos was steered by her mother toward the convent. Her freewheeling father left a distinct imprint. In a time when two thirds of women couldn't even sign their names, Henri de Lenclos saw to it that his darling "Ninon" learned her letters. He set the stage for her libertine philosophy. "Utilize precious time, and have no scruples about the quantity of your pleasures, but only of their quality," he advised from his deathbed. In Marion de Rambouillet's famous Blue Room salon, Ninon was launched as a courtesan in Parisian society.

The exquisite Marion didn't quite *get*, at first, that her plainer friend was a Siren—until Ninon stole Marion's lover out from under her powdered nose. Ninon's appeal was not her beauty, "of which she never had much," but her affectionate and stimulating company. Her lively mind always "attune[s] itself to who she is with. . . ." She was a particularly engaging and provocative conversationalist.

"Reserve delicacy of sentiment for friendship; accept love for what it is. . . . The more dignity you give it, the more dangerous you make it."

—*Ninon de Lenclos*

"I notice that the most frivolous things are charged up to the account of women," said twenty-year-old Ninon. "From this moment, I will be a man." She rejected marriage as an "odious" tyranny. Of course, there was always the nasty business of how a girl on her own would live. She divided her admiring legions into "payeurs" (those who paid for her company but not necessarily sex), "martyrs" (those who struck out), and her "favorites," all of whom flocked to her salon to hear her play her lute. Her carefully chosen "caprices" (love affairs) rarely exceeded three months. "Love with passion but only for a few minutes," she said. Once tossed from her bed, her lovers were reinstated as lifelong friends—and as a Companion Siren, of course, she had many of those. Miffed by Ninon's drawing power, French Queen Anne had her locked in a convent. Queen Christina of Sweden came to her rescue.

"In seventeenth-century Paris, Ninon de Lenclos was the last word in the court of public opinion," wrote her biographer. King Louis XIV wouldn't think of changing mistresses without asking, "What does Ninon think?" She abhorred "virtue" in the traditional or religious sense, but set high standards for romantic etiquette. "It takes more skill to make love than to command an army," she said. Men were apparently so wanting on love's battlefields that Ninon opened a School of Gallantry to set them straight. Her lectures covered the psychology of women, the techniques of courting and seduction, and—oh, my—an exploratory course in the physiology of sex. She occasionally went in for a little lab work.

NINON DE LENCLOS, ON HER LAST BIRTHDAY

by Dorothy Parker

So let me have the rouge again,

And comb my hair the curly way.

The poor young men, the dear young men

They'll be here at noon today.

I shall wear the blue, I think—

They beg to touch its rippled lace;

Or do they love me best in pink,

So sweetly flattering the face?

And are you sure my eyes are bright,

And is it true my cheek is clear?

Young what's-his-name stayed half the night;

He vows to cut his throat, poor dear!

So bring my scarlet slippers, then,

And fetch the powder-puff to me.

The dear young men, the poor young men

—They think I'm only seventy!

"To be received with open arms, you must be agreeable, amusing, and necessary to the pleasure of others," she advised a young pupil. Ninon had no patience with braggarts or pedants. She taught that women sometimes said "no" when they meant "Yes!"—politically incorrect today, but radical in its time. Seeing his opening, her twenty-three-year-old student promptly threw himself at his forty-eight-year-old mistress. It's even been reported that Ninon's natural son fell for his mother, and then messily took his life at the discovery of who she was.

In late middle age, Ninon presided over her salon as the stately "Mademoiselle de Lenclos," advisor on matters of the heart. In her swan song, she promised a randy young *abbé* a night of unbridled pleasure. The night she finally succumbed, she claimed it was her eightieth birthday present to herself.

Ninon's Lesson

Ninon "exercised all the rights and privileges of the male sex," without ever neglecting her substantial feminine charms. Her lovers may have paid the bills, but Ninon refused to be bought—and said so in no uncertain terms. She lived as she saw fit and was beholden to no one. To her many amorous admirers, Ninon's independent thinking was the sexiest part of her.

TAKE THE HIGH ROAD

Forced to flee France, a friend of Ninon's turned over half his fortune in a casket to her for safekeeping. The rest he entrusted to a priest. When he returned, guess who gave him back his cash with interest and who no longer had a penny of it? Voltaire dubbed Ninon "the beautiful keeper of the casket," in a legend of honor that has been often repeated throughout history. To earn a "place in the ranks of illustrious men," strive to be the "man of honor" that Ninon was. Don't welsh on a bet, stab a friend in the back, or scramble to get in the lifeboat first.

How did a pretty-ish girl from nowhere pull such weight in French society? It would seem about as likely as Britney Spears becoming U.S. Chief of Protocol. The secret was in Ninon's exceptional character. She strove to be an *homme honnête* (literally, honest man)—whose solemn word could be counted on. She stood by her philosophy of free love even when it became inconvenient to her. On learning that her lover was romancing her friend, she scolded them not for their actions but for sneaking around. It was said that the more one pondered the "merits of Ninon," the more attractive she became. The conviction behind her unconventional thinking melted their hearts.

Too many great ladies of today strive to fit the mold. I won't name names, but you know who you are. Have you noticed how the admired actresses of Hollywood have predictable opinions of the world? Courtney Love almost comes as a relief. It makes me wonder what Gretchen, a former classmate, is doing today. Always a charmer, Gretchen trod an independent path, even in grade school. We elected her class president year after year. While the rest of us were plotting our way to the prom, Gretchen was digging up ruins on a remote island in Greece. Men (really boys) fell all over themselves with admiration for her. She could have taken her pick of any of them. And had she demanded they wear skirts, they would have taken it seriously. Why? Like Ninon, Gretchen's thinking was deep and true. Her "rules" were always a carefully considered expression of who she was at core.

In any century, a woman with an independent mind has the power to bewitch—never more so than today. To lay siege to their hearts, you must first command their wholehearted respect. But remember, you'll never do it with a sledge-hammer and megaphone. Work out the terms of your philosophy in the Siren way. To paraphrase Simone de Beauvoir: to the women who exploit their femininity "to the limit" go the spoils.

Is a School of Gallantry in your future? *You*, my dear, will have no trouble calling the shots if you know exactly what you think and why. Be true to yourself, even if your line of reasoning isn't particularly fashionable. Show them the measure of your character. Don't change your mind midstream just because the water gets murky and cold. Move serenely like a proud schooner, and they'll hear your Siren call in the fog.

play the field

Zelda Sayre Fitzgerald

1900–1948

Companion/Competitor Siren

"Hurry back to Montgomery as town is shot to pieces since you left," Zelda Sayre's Southern beaus wired her in New York. "No pep. No fun. No one to give the gossipers a source of conversation. . . ." True to form, the new Mrs. F. Scott Fitzgerald was busy riding on taxi tops and diving into public fountains, champagne glass first—in other words, giving the Roaring Twenties its reputation for daring and decadence. The Fitzgeralds were a "beautiful apparition," riding high on the crest of Scott's literary fame. The novel *This Side of Paradise* had just been published, and Zelda—the "first American flapper"—was its inspiration. But marriage to the man of the hour didn't stop Zelda from breaking hearts from New York to the French Riviera.

Before the fictional exploits of Scarlett O'Hara were detailed in *Gone With the Wind*, real-life Zelda Sayre scandalized the Eastern corridor. She smoked cigarettes, told shocking stories, danced cheek-to-cheek, and wore a flesh-colored bathing suit—racy stuff, believe me, for a debutante in those charmed pre-war years. Southern belles were chaste and demure or, at the very least, pretended to be. Of "two kinds of girls, those who would ride with you in your automobile at night, and the nice girls who wouldn't," Zelda Sayre was decidedly the first. If Montgomery talked, who gave a damn? Zelda thrived on it.

Beautiful Zelda had a voracious appetite for life. She literally dove from dizzying heights into the icy water below. Her Competitor Siren's nerve and defiance gave her swains the giddy feeling that things might spin deliriously out of control. The boys flocked like delighted rubber-neckers to the accident scene. The rush

itself was part of her buzz. At Alabama's Auburn University, five football play-ers formed "Zeta Sigma" fraternity in Zelda's honor, and its initiates were known for their "rabid devotion" to their Montgomery belle. Aviators at the nearby mil-itary base did dangerous stunts overhead to impress her.

"Nobody has ever measured, not even poets, how much the heart can hold."

—*Zelda Fitzgerald*

When Scott met Zelda at a country club dance in 1918, he was stationed nearby at the war's end. Their alchemy was instant. "There seemed to be some heavenly support beneath his shoulder blades that lifted his feet from the ground in some ecstatic suspension," she said of their dance. From those words, you can well imagine why the budding novelist shamelessly lifted from Zelda's diaries for his prose. When Fitzgerald returned north to make his literary name, the romance flickered on and off. "I will not, shall not, can not, should not, must not marry," Scott wrote to a friend. Not prepared to pine, Zelda boasted that she had "kissed thousands of men" and intended "to kiss thousands more." If this was part of her plan to keep Scott under her spell, it was diabolical.

"Darling, I love you more than anything in the world," she wrote Scott in New York. It didn't stop her from smooching an aviator to find out how his mustache felt. When her beloved failed to write, what else could she do? She succumbed to the charms of a young man who had landed in town for a golfing event. Then there was the weekend that Zelda's exploits made society headlines in the Montgomery *and* Atlanta papers: she left Alabama wearing her picturesque Leghorn hat with streamers, it was reported, and was met at the station by no fewer than four men from Georgia Tech—each of whom had booked her as his date. That weekend, Zelda got "stewed" and then "pinned," even though she was semi-betrothed to Scott at that point.

"I am in love with a whirlwind," Fitzgerald wrote, "and I must spin a net big enough to catch it." When she switched a letter meant for Scott with one she intended for another man, he'd had enough. Scott was on the next train to Montgomery with a proposal of marriage. "The girl worth having won't wait," he wrote.

Hey, but didn't Zelda finally do a triple off the deep end? And wasn't F. Scott Fitzgerald that writer who drank way, way too much? Their doomed but romantic story is great literary stuff. In my family, we never let a *soupçon* of insanity ruin a seductress's tale. Zelda Sayre Fitzgerald was the great Siren of the Jazz Age. In the gracious Southern tradition, her candy coating disguised nerves of steel. If there's one thing a Southern Belle learns at her mother's knee, it's how to look like a lady, while keeping a man or two in reserve.

Zelda's Lesson

College boys she barely knew kept Zelda's picture tacked on their walls. One man thought they were dating right up until he read in the newspapers that she'd married Scott. She belonged to herself and "to the crowd, rather than any single suitor," Fitzgerald would write in "The Debutante." Instinctively she knew that part of her attractiveness for Scott was her allure for every other man in the room. Even as Mrs. F. Scott Fitzgerald, she fielded love notes and poetry, shamelessly working her popularity. Fearless and fun, Zelda was a shooting star, with an uncanny "ability to manage men without ever seeming to." She mastered the fine art of playing the field.

In my hometown (south of the Mason Dixon line), we had two reigning bachelors who were forever eluding the intricate matrimonial webs of our local belles. Their "fear of commitment" had become legendary. Or so girls told themselves. Then along came Stephanie—a Siren from the North!—who, like Sherman in Atlanta, burned her way into the hearts of both men. She had them vying so frantically for her attention that she took to leaving her phone off the hook. She wouldn't give up either until one proposed, and jaws dropped when one finally did. Was she "romancing" two men, to put it gingerly? For all I know, it was a sexual revolving door through the week and into the weekend. Believe me, it wouldn't have been a hardship. Maybe she was saving herself for the wedding night. I never asked, but Stephanie sure was a lesson in effective management.

LEAVE INCRIMINATING EVIDENCE

Did Zelda switch her letter to Scott with one for his rival by accident? We'll never know, but it sure got his attention. It won't do *you* any good to play the field if he never gets wind of it. Take a tip from Zelda. Let him know you're in hot demand. There's no need to brag—anyway, it's unladylike. Just get a little careless with the incriminating evidence: that e-mail open on your screen, the card that came with the flowers, the voicemail you couldn't quite stifle quickly enough. Assure him that these men mean nothing to you—they just can't help themselves.

Whatever happened to the fine Southern tradition of collecting beaus? It didn't mean a woman was a cheatin' Lucille, it just meant she was keeping her options open until she knew what was what or until someone fabulous came along. Then, playing the field kept Mr. Fabulous on his toes. Women are far too eager today to forfeit their freedom for a commitment of some kind—sometimes even before checking for back hair or even if he's married to someone else. He won't thank you for your sacrifice, ladies, as my mother used to say. You may even leave him with the impression that you're a little *too* available. He's certainly not sitting at home waiting for *you* to call. You lose your leverage instantly.

A Siren should have that powerful feeling that she's wanted in at least three states—by men who would swoop her up in an instant if they could. There's no point in denying what's Human Nature 101—competition is a market maker. What's perceived as desirable becomes even more so. Never stop playing the field completely, even when you're part of a team.

ARE YOU THINKING LIKE A MAN? (IN MATTERS OF THE HEART)

It's not a call to arms. No need to put aside your beguiling femininity. Thinking like a man only means you behave strategically in matters of the heart. If your answer to the questions below is more often "yes" than "no," you could be the sexy Siren who calls the shots.

✦ Do you think of yourself as master of your own romantic fate?

✦ Is the double standard in gender relations a relic of the past?

✦ Do you think men respond well to independence in women?

✦ Do you go after what you want without worrying about whether it looks "right"?

✦ Do you think it's possible for a very feminine woman to be as powerful as a man?

✦ Do you see yourself as more of a "Virgin Queen" than a "Dutiful Wife"?

✦ Do you feel that it's advisable to keep your romantic options open until you know a lot about a man you're considering becoming involved with?

✦ Is the woman who lives by her own rules happier than the one who looks for guidance?

✦ Is it human nature to want what you can't have?

✦ Do you agree that a woman who allows herself all the "privileges and pleasures" of a man should take the hits without complaint?

Build Your Power Base

What's behind the irresistible Siren's call? It's her talent for being an individual. What she does, she does to the max. The Siren makes her mark on the world—which, in turn, renders her that much more irresistible. In one man's words, "a woman who has qualities that put me in awe is far more likely to make me think she is worth falling for."

A Siren polishes her particular talents and strengths until they glow. She puts her energy into being unabashedly strong, wherever it may lead. She may be a rebel with a cause or a beauty with the brains to solve the thorniest political issues. She may blow them away by singing a song that speaks to their hearts. She lives large, offers up her ripest fruit, and has more than enough charisma to light the way. In this chapter, you'll meet just a few of the Sirens who were experts at developing their power base.

Under a street lamp in a working-class neighborhood of Paris, Edith Piaf was born on the cusp of World War I. She was an unlikely Siren who lured them literally with the power of her song. Clare Boothe Luce never rested on the laurels of a pretty face. She captured the hearts of trophy men with her fiery intellect. And what's not to love about Susan Sarandon? She fights for what's right—and in the process she's become the smart man's fantasy seductress. Through their lessons, the aspiring Siren can live and learn.

Radical chic . . . or chic radical?

be a rebel with a cause

Susan Sarandon

(née Susan Abigail Tomalin)

1946–

Mother Siren

In the movie *Thelma & Louise*, Susan Sarandon and Geena Davis hot-foot it to Mexico in a vintage green convertible. What starts out as a weekend away from their deadbeat men spins way out of control. They are wanted in two states—traveling just an hour or two ahead of the law. These gorgeous desperados are long past regret. There's nothing left for them at home. The trucker who's been gesturing obscenely in their direction on the highway is about to get more than he bargained for. Luring him off the road with a tease, Thelma punctures his tires with a revolver. Louise detonates his truck into volcanic bits. For every woman who's dealt with pond scum like him, the scene is sweet retribution, a vicarious thrill. They are Siren rebels in designer shades.

Sarandon (Louise) is the repressed mother hen, with a prim little up-do and a knack for spoiling fun. All, naturally, is not as it appears at first. Louise is pushing the horror of being raped out of her head, quashing a seething rage that's bound to explode. Sarandon is at her most provocative when she's evening the score. It's the kind of role she was born to play. From her earliest reckoning, she had "a highly developed sense of justice." Today, her Siren image depends on it.

Susan Abigail Tomalin grew up the oldest of nine—a Mother Siren with a running start. She married actor Chris Sarandon in college, when "living together" still shocked the establishment. In one of those as-fate-would-have-it tales, Chris brought her along to an audition, and wide-eyed Susan's career was launched. *Pretty Baby* and *The Rocky Horror Picture Show* put her on the map, but the full-court Siren was yet to come. Post-divorce, she was squired by directors like Franco Amurri and Louis Malle. Her career was stalled at ingénue.

As a meddling housewife in *Compromising Positions*, Sarandon was touted as delectable. That voice was spiked milk with a cinnamon twist. It wasn't until she was cast as the slinky mother figure in *Bull Durham* that her ship reached port. Sarandon was forty—yikes, practically over the hill—and had been discounted as too old for the part. Her audition changed everything. As Annie Savoy, she was a "sexual missionary," a small-town teacher who worships at the altar of baseball. Annie turns a young pitcher (Tim Robbins) into an ace by plying him with kinky sex and Walt Whitman's verse. "Sarandon is so irresistible in the part," wrote a critic, "it may not strike you until afterward that she's a total male fantasy." The Mother Siren often takes the stealth approach.

After the film, Sarandon took her twenty-eight-year-old co-star home. The couple became a kind of Bonnie and Clyde to conservatives. Haitian refugees, world hunger, civil rights, AIDS victims, women's issues, and the Gulf wars, Sarandon stands her ground for peace and the underdog. "She's the most liberal person I've ever met in my life," said one of her staunchest admirers. Asked if she thinks her views have sometimes hurt her career, she says, "that's like worrying whether your slip is showing while you flee a burning building." Actually, a trip downtown in the paddy wagon only seems to help. "Her manifest intelligence, political activism, and ripe sensuality make her a thinking man's object of desire," wrote a film critic, "but she's never been reduced to sex appeal alone."

Sarandon can gain twenty pounds and do a boozy waitress with bags under her eyes—*White Palace*—and still seduce. She can look decidedly "lived in" (to use her words), and pull off the "nurturing voluptuary" about whom men fantasize. As the snarling she-wolf, Sarandon shows them that there is more to womanhood than looking good.

Susan's Lesson

In *Dead Man Walking*, Sarandon explored the death penalty. In public service announcements, she's fought for First Amendment rights and gays in Hollywood. She's lectured from the pulpit of the Academy Awards—and taken the stage to protest police brutality at a rally in Central Park. She's done time more than once in the name of public outrage and sisterhood. The world loves a heroine—particularly one who's willing to suffer for the fight. A few knocks never hurt a rebel on the rise. Look at Joan of Arc—she was *nothing* if not a Siren willing to take the heat for her cause. It's no accident that she's been played by some of the most glamorous women in Hollywood.

CHOOSE AN ALLURING CAUSE

There really is a cause called Puppies Behind Bars, but joining it is not likely to up your Siren appeal. And Save the Whales if you like, but don't expect it to win romantic points. It's the epic moral issues that come with cachet—and the liberal route is always preferable. It's way sexier to be working against the establishment than for it. Fight for peace, African wildlife, anything green and sustainable. Stand up for the oppressed anywhere on the globe. But to fight the good fight, you've got to believe. Choose the cause you truly think is worthiest.

There's something decidedly sexy about a woman who *believes*. And by believe, I don't mean that the "End Will Come." Or even in the presence of weapons of mass destruction in the absence of evidence. You've got to stand up for the do-or-die cause with all the courage you can muster from the roiling depths of your soul—that is, if you want to be the rebel Siren who gets his knickers in a twist. In the seventies, Vanessa Redgrave and Julie Christie made radical chic. Brad was smitten by Angelina's desire to save the world. In and out of the bedroom, the passionate woman sends an arrow to his heart. Just remember to crack a smile as you go.

On Manhattan's Upper West Side, there's a hard-bitten woman who hawks

animal rights from the sidewalk. In Midtown, a grim conga line called Women Dressed in Black protests something I've never quite been able to get a handle on. These are women not likely to win converts to their cause, unless it's saving the doughty from mid-calf skirts. Why is Sarandon the Siren rebel who turns men on? Because she gets that "radical messages in good-looking pop bottles" go down easier. On Sarandon, protest was never so persuasive or glamorous.

Fight for human rights and environmental protection. Rush to the site of the accident. Grab a cameraman and get your buns to a war zone, à la Amanpour. When you arrive, take your cause—but not yourself—dead seriously. Remember to consult hair and wardrobe. Don't be such a saint (or martyr) that they can't see the delicious sinner in you. The Siren rebel is all passionate bidness, until it's time to call it quits for the day. Then, you might find her teaching Jude Law how to drink absinthe straight up.

Worry about the state of the world, because that's precisely what they dig about you. But get the facts and the issues straight. During the Vietnam War, Jane Fonda blew her Siren cool (we love her anyway) by managing to look like she was rooting for the other side. Honey attracts more flies than vinegar, you've heard, so there's no harm in being a glamour puss. You're a saleswoman, in the very best sense of the word. Your courage and conviction are sponsored by Cover Girl.

hone your talent

CASE STUDY:

Edith Piaf

(née Gassion)

1915–1963

Sex Kitten/Mother Siren

"Look at this little creature, her hands like a lizard among the ruins . . . eyes full of wonder like a blind man who can suddenly see," wrote playwright Jean Cocteau. "How will she sing? How will she squeeze those great wails of the night out of that narrow breast? Have you heard a nightingale? She labors, hesitates, rasps, chokes. And then, suddenly, she sings. You are entranced."

With arms outstretched, Edith Piaf sang of the fleeting triumphs of love, then abandonment, and the harshness of fate. It was *As the World Turns*—in French—without the upscale clothes. Her moon face pale and wan, Piaf was the eternal street urchin, even at the height of her popularity. Her lyrics, cresting on top of her voice's jagged edge, reached deep into the soul and spoke of a universal angst. "She gave performances that drove men crazy," wrote a critic. They "leaned forward in their seats as though they wanted to take her in their arms." Men showered Piaf with the admiration she craved, and left their wives steaming at home.

"A voice like hers comes along once in a century," wrote her sister. "She didn't force herself to be 'realistic.'" Edith Gassion was born in the working-class streets she sang of—literally on a policeman's cloak under a street lamp. She took her act on the road, first as a sidekick to her acrobat father, and then with her half sister, Simone. The two bedraggled little dames sang their hearts out on street corners to a captivated "raft of men." A nightclub owner turned Edith into *La Môme Piaf*—The Kid Sparrow. Soon her fame was international; her lyrics to hit songs like *La Vie en Rose* and *Non, Je Ne Regrette Rien* were no doubt practiced in shower stalls

all over the globe. American audiences were at first baffled by the French waif, then sold. "Piaf is the best champagne salesman in the U.S.," wrote a critic. "The minute she sings in a nightclub, your throat gets dry with emotion."

"I never saw a man who could resist Edith," wrote her sister. Unless she was dead drunk, she required a man's "leg next to hers" in bed at night. It was a revolving door—her sister considered assigning numbers to keep them all straight. "I've got sagging breasts, a low-slung ass, and little drooping buttocks," Edith said. "But I can still get men." Piaf racked up lovers and demanded that they play by her rules—among them, singers Charles Aznavour, Yves Montand, and Jacques Pils. Her "true love" was the boxer Marcel Cerdan, deified after his plane crashed in the Azores. For Piaf, love might last only twenty-four hours—tops, no more than two or three years. Her mantra was "a woman who gets herself dropped is a poor sap. There's no lack of men . . . find a replacement."

"When love gets lukewarm, you either have to heat it up or chuck it. Love doesn't keep on ice!"

—*Edith Piaf*

Piaf liked to dress and "educate" her men. She knit them sweaters that didn't fit. She was a Mother Siren catastrophically short on housekeeping skills. It was the "classy" lover who introduced her to the hygienic wonders of a toothbrush. In love, Piaf "ate her heart out . . . was jealous and possessive . . . had doubts . . . howled . . . locked her guys up . . . and cheated on them," wrote her sister. All things considered, she was "unbearable." Yet her "mesmeric Siren song" with its Kittenish tale of innocence gone wrong proved irresistible.

Spent and drug-addicted, the Little Sparrow was still drawing them up on the rocks near the end with her Siren song. Her last husband of three, a cutie-pie singer named Theo Sarapo, was half her age. "He didn't notice that Edith's hands were all knotted up," said her sister, "or that she looked like she had lived one hundred years."

I've believed too much, too much, too much,
All that street-corner claptrap,
People have told me so many times, I've heard so many times,
"I adore you" and "For the rest of my life."
What was it all for? Who was it all for?
I thought I'd seen everything,
Done everything, said everything, heard everything,
And I said to myself: "I won't be fooled again!"
And then he came along!

—*J'en ai tant vu, tant vu* by Michel Emer with René Rouzzaud

Edith's Lesson

On an American tour, Piaf collapsed from hard living and alcohol. A handsome young admirer sent violets and was ushered to her hospital bedside. Piaf looked like the tail end of a misspent life—which is what she was. "He didn't give a damn about her drawn, ravaged face, her skinny arms, her huge bare forehead, her sickly looking skin," wrote Piaf's sister. He went on seeing her as if she were still on stage, in all the magic of the spotlights. "Her beauty lay in her talent"—and that talent transformed.

"Talent is like electricity," said the poet Maya Angelou. "We don't understand electricity. We use it—to light up a lamp, keep a heart pump going, light a cathedral. . . ." Talent attracts, sometimes the multitudes. Without talent—let's face it—little Edith Gassion from Pigalle wouldn't have generated enough heat to set off a smoke alarm. Her talent was so big that the pint-sized girl with the "Punchinello face" was lifted into the Siren's realm.

It's no news that talent is sexy. Since ancient times, women have used their talents to ensnare, along with beauty, brains, and sex. Her talent gilds the lily; whatever she was to start with, it makes her more in his eyes. Piaf's "talent compensated for a lot of things," wrote her sister. We know it's true. In our wildest dreams, what are we doing? Singing to the masses, painting a masterpiece, or writing great prose. We believe that talent will bring us riches, admiration, and love. And it will. We've all seen it happen dozens of times.

LEARN TO JUGGLE

Maybe you don't sing like a nightingale, paint like Picasso, or write like the author of *Pride and Prejudice*. (Or, more power to you, maybe you do.) It's time to pick up a party trick. Find something somewhat hard to do—like juggling—and practice until you master it. Opportunities will abound to display your skill. You watch. Men will be more than a little impressed.

"Every person is born with talent," believes Angelou. It's your job to figure out what for. Be aware that talent can take many, many forms and still lure. My cousin's athletic grace always sweeps men away—though it's hard for women to understand why. Maybe you're a whiz at the clever toast, the inventor of brilliant financial instruments, or can twist a piece of aluminum foil into designer evening clothes. Hone what you do well until it's shiny and sure. Then hide it under "a beautiful veil of modesty" to attract even more.

develop your mind

Clare Boothe Luce

1903–1987

Goddess/Competitor Siren

At a party in New York in the summer of 1932, Clare Boothe staked out Henry Luce—a man who considered himself the intellectual inferior of no one. "Clare was far too clever to appear impressed with him," remembered the hostess. She leaned casually into the curve of the piano, tossed off witty remarks, and laughed as if she had not a care in the world. She baited Luce, the founder of Time Inc., with criticisms of *Fortune*. She boldly proposed the photo-illustrated format for what became *Life* magazine. Abruptly, Luce consulted his pocket watch and cut the conversation short, leaving Clare to fume. She had never been treated so indifferently. Yet the next time they met—at a party at the Waldorf—Luce decided within minutes of conversation to leave his wife. He claimed it was a *coup de foudre*—a stroke of lightning. Luce said he had found his long-sought cerebral twin in Clare.

Clare Boothe could have gotten by on her incandescent looks alone. The "magical loveliness" of her gaze and her porcelain skin were unforgettable. But her ambition was to "climb high in the world of men" and dazzle them with her accomplishments. At the time she met Luce, she was editor of *Vanity Fair* and had published her witty essays as *Stuffed Shirts*. She went on to write hit Broadway plays and a shrewd history of the Allies before World War II. At the height of her powers, Clare won two terms in Congress and became President Eisenhower's ambassador to Italy. To hear her tell it, she gave Churchill the phrase "blood, sweat, and tears" and named FDR's New Deal. Along the way, she bedded some of the world's richest and most powerful men, who prized her brilliance above all.

Boothe's mother never married her father—the family shame—and supported the family, essentially, as a call girl. A rich husband for Clare was their ticket out, if she could just be persuaded to keep it quiet. "Don't talk heavy stuff to them," her mother urged. "Never let them see what makes the wheels go round." Clare preferred the Goddess route. At twenty, she landed George Tuttle Brokaw, an older, alcoholic scion of New York society. Her flirtations drove him nearly mad. He put her up on a pedestal. His generous divorce settlement five years later freed Clare to become a career girl—just for kicks. She showed up at *Vogue*, sat at a desk, and wrote captions until they cried "uncle" and gave her a paycheck.

"If God had wanted us to think with our wombs, why did he give us a brain?"

—Clare Boothe Luce

"I prefer being alone with brilliant men," said Clare. There was no shortage of applicants. She juggled three or four suitors in any given month, all of whom were captivated by her superior mind. At *Vanity Fair*, she romanced her editor, who played Pygmalion to his rising star. He installed an Underwood typewriter in their love nest and prodded her on. "As soon as he got me on my feet, he wanted me on my back," she joked. Condé Nast, *Vanity Fair*'s publisher, lusted after his "intellectual showpiece." "Blinded" by her nimble mind, financier Bernard Baruch called her the "best female intellect."

In love, Clare stuck to a single-minded Goddess Siren philosophy: "There's only one way of keeping love alive—starve it!" Writer Paul Gallico turned obsessive after Clare canceled a date. He wasn't the first to observe that she pulled back from his declarations of love, only to come around at his retreat. She didn't value the man who "made himself too easily available." The love "most likely to last" for La Boothe was the kind that went unreturned.

"A woman's best protection is the right man," she wrote in her play *The Women*. Henry Luce had a vast fortune, an intellectual empire, a pedigree. He was the kind of husband she had always dreamed of, even if she wasn't exactly in love with him. During their affair—a secret to no one—Clare became Luce's "idea person." She pored over *Time* and *Fortune*, sending him detailed memos of improvements. She had an innate feel for page layout. Their pillow talk was all world events and clever word games, sometimes lasting until dawn. The star-struck Luce eagerly showcased her brilliance. When Luce briefly questioned leaving his wife, Clare disappeared. Her ploy worked. "If ever there was the slightest doubt about my divorce," he wrote, "I can have none now." In 1935, they married in a quiet ceremony.

The Luce marriage survived Clare's ambitions—and indiscretions—not always happily. He was forever begging for his wife's attention or asking her to return from across the world. "I love you," she wrote. "Forgive me for not proving it by living with you more." Luce's wealthy widow went out as a member of President Reagan's Foreign Intelligence Advisory Board.

Clare's Lesson

Clare's "sinewy" mind was an integral part of her sex appeal. To Luce, her razzle-dazzle intellect was "adorable." If she hadn't been driven to reduce him to a stuttering fool, she might have been the ultimate companion to any man at the top of his game. Clare had to prove that she was far more than Luce's mental match; she was vastly superior. To their dismay, *Life* editors perceived her as "the real boss" of the show. Socially, she held court, relegating Luce to a functionary role. When he "failed" in bed—with ever-increasing frequency—she delighted in broadcasting the news.

MEASURE YOUR WORDS

Sometimes it's better to close your mouth and be thought a fool, than to open it and remove all doubt—an old adage that's always excellent advice. Don't be so eager to look bright that you push crackpot opinions on subjects about which you are ill-informed. If you want to look smarter in general, linguist Deborah Tannen suggests speeding up your speech. Also banish words that don't mean anything. "Uh-huh" and "hmm" sound better as "sure" and "of course." And never use the word "like" except as a verb or a metaphor.

Two decades ago, *Newsweek* reported that a smart, successful woman out of her thirties was more likely to be singled out by a terrorist than to marry. Where did that come from? Women rushed to dumb it down. Men mourned their sudden lack of backbone. In 2006, *Why Smart Men Marry Smart Women* reported that ninety percent of high-achieving men want a woman with brains—which sounds like the men I know. Men do *more* than make passes at girls who wear glasses. "A woman who has qualities that put me in awe," confided one man to *Times* columnist Maureen Dowd, "is far more likely to make me think she is worth falling for."

If that's the case, then why does the myth persist that men like 'em dumb? Well, some do of course. And there's no question that the mute *Playboy* babe fantasy strikes a chord. But as far back as anyone can remember, men have been turned on by smart talk; in sixteenth-century Venice they were even willing to pay for it. They are not looking for a woman who can't connect the dots. But *nobody* likes a woman who thinks her brains are all that count in the world. "I certainly don't want my home life to reflect the sorry state of American corporate life," a man wrote Dowd, where everyone thinks that he/she is so damned smart that they "rarely do anything of consequence for anyone."

At best, Clare Boothe offered up her superior mind as a delightful gift—at worst, it was a blunt instrument. You could call her life a cautionary, as well as an inspirational, tale. In the final analysis, a smart woman without "central heating"—à la Boothe—undercuts her Siren goals. Earn your Ph.D. in quantum physics. Write the history of the world. Cure cancer, or give new meaning to stem cell research. But don't go thinking you're God's gift, girl.

Superiority is intolerable in him; don't imagine it's fetching on you. Nobody wants to cozy up to someone who acts as though she's suffering fools. He's looking for a friend, not a foe. Critical thinking is sexy, as long as it's not for taking inventory of his faults.

ARE YOU BUILDING YOUR POWER BASE?

Are you unafraid to be the best that you are, or do you neglect the qualities that make you remarkable? Flaunt what you got, and take it as far as it goes. Ponder the questions below. If you can answer most in the affirmative, then your power base is strong.

+ Do you think achievement makes a woman more, rather than less, desirable to men?
+ Are you able to assess your strengths objectively?
+ Do you make the most of your talents?
+ Do you tend to be passionate about what you believe?
+ Are you willing to fight for what matters to you?
+ Do you think smart men like smart women?
+ Do you pursue a line of work that makes the most of what you have to offer?
+ Do you operate at the top of your game?

Cautionary Tales

Anne Boleyn—was she an adulteress or the victim of the madness of King Henry VIII? If she'd just been a little less greedy, she might have lived to a prosperous old age. The infamous Mary Queen of Scots was a fool for love. All her troubles came from refusing to see the truth. The daughter of a pope, Lucrezia Borgia was the pawn of her family. Her reputation suffered from allowing herself to be pushed around.

Think of them as the harridan, the hopeless romantic, and the pushover. They were among the most seductive women in history, yet they squandered their power by losing perspective. Playing your Siren cards wrong during the Renaissance could cost you your head—as it did in the cases of both Anne and Mary.

While the names of these Sirens are familiar, where they went wrong is less so. Their stories are cautionary tales. They show us how and where modern Sirens can get off track. Don't let history repeat itself in your life. Attend to the lessons of some of the world's most powerful seductresses, whose fatal flaws led to their downfall.

don't get greedy

CASE STUDY:

Anne Boleyn

1504?–1536

Goddess Siren

In the bleak winter of 1536, the long-awaited son of Anne Boleyn and King Henry VIII arrived prematurely, stillborn. With this blow, Henry was finished with Anne, the woman he'd overturned his kingdom to marry just three years before. Yet, in her wildest dreams, Anne could not have imagined how the King would get rid of her. Arrested on trumped-up charges of adultery and incest, she was swiftly tried, convicted, and sentenced to death. Until the end, she expected mercy that did not come. "I pray God save the king and send him long to reign over you," said Boleyn, uncharacteristically gracious in her final hour. "And thus I take my leave of the world and of you all." With that, she was beheaded in the first public execution of an English Queen.

Anne Boleyn began her climb to the throne as a lady-in-waiting to Catherine of Aragon, Henry's first Queen. From the moment she set her dainty foot on English soil, Anne stood out. Polished in French courts, she was admired for her wit, sophistication, and chic. Though no beauty, she had masses of black, glossy hair and used her expressive eyes "to great effect"—moving Henry Percy, future Earl of Northumberland, to propose. The King flew into a rage when he heard. Anne was sent home to Hever Castle, where she fumed, at which point Henry began dropping by for tea. Would she be his mistress if he pledged his allegiance to her alone? Thanks, but no thanks, said Anne. It will be Queen or nothing at all.

Anne knew how these things went down. Her sister, Mary—"the other Boleyn girl"—was *her* cautionary tale. As the King's one-time mistress, Mary had no property or riches to show for her trouble, only an unsavory reputation for

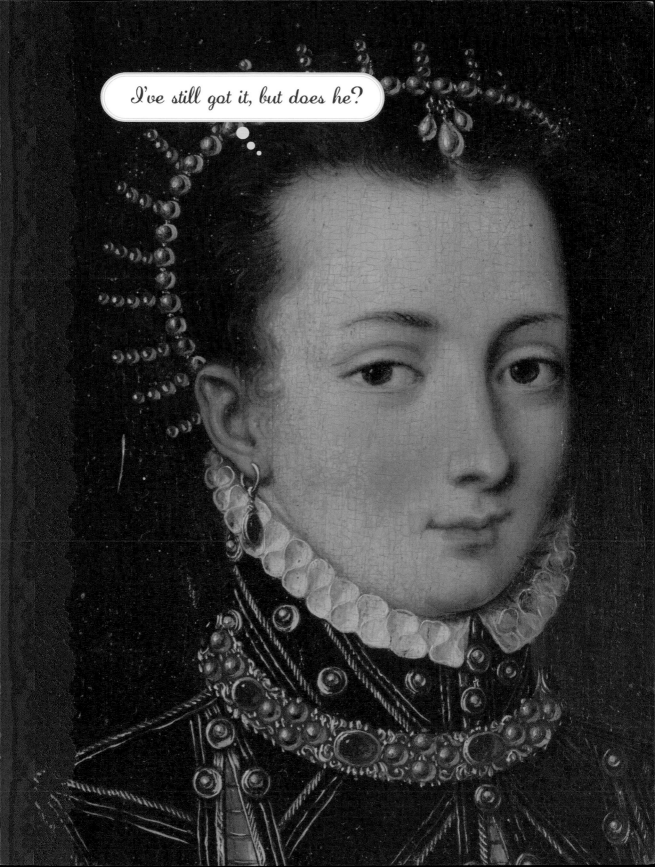

sleeping around. Anne knew that Henry's "vagrant fancy, soon satisfied, would have burned itself out." For Henry, who was accustomed to getting his way, anything out of reach was positively irresistible. By holding the King at arm's length—which, incredibly, Anne did for *seven* years—she became an obsession for which he was willing to pay any price. Anne never doubted her right to the spoils. Her arrogance, of course, would be her downfall.

NEED TO KNOW DEPT.

Anne Boleyn had two birthmarks, or deformities, cited as evidence of witchcraft. One was a mole the size of a strawberry below her right ear (the "Devil's Pawmark"), the second was at the beginning of a sixth finger on her right hand, which she hid with the tips of her other fingers and by wearing long sleeves. This is rumored to be one of the reasons King Henry VIII wrote "Greensleeves" for her.

In his quest to get Anne into bed, Henry banished long-suffering Catherine of Aragon to the hinterlands. When the Pope refused him an annulment, Henry broke his ties with the Catholic Church, anointed himself leader of the new Church of England, and received his orders directly from God. And God, apparently, had Anne Boleyn in mind for the throne. Those who were with Henry said "aye" quickly. Those who were against him ended up with their heads on spikes; many of them had been his closest friends and advisors. For centuries to come, this split would become the cause of bloody strife between Catholics and Protestants, from which we're still reeling today. Henry—so charming in his youth—became increasingly ruthless and paranoid.

Famous for his six wives, King Henry VIII next married Jane Seymour, Anne's lady-in-waiting, who died after giving birth to a son. A royal mail-order bride, Anne of Cleves, followed, but she didn't turn him on. She survived the axe only by agreeing to have the marriage annulled. He beheaded sixteen-year-old Katherine Howard, also on charges of adultery. Henry died not long after marrying Katherine Parr. The great Elizabeth I, Anne Boleyn's daughter by Henry, eventually became Queen.

Anne's Lesson

For Anne, landing Henry was never a question of love. She was peeved over the slights she had suffered from her relatively minor status at court, and she'd been denied Henry Percy—or as she said, "sooner Harry's countess than Henry's Queen." Anne vowed to get revenge, once she had the power to throw her weight around. She was a Siren motivated almost entirely by greed.

Anne suffered not a moment's remorse over the banishment of saintly Catherine, who had been Queen for more than twenty years. She all but ordered the beheadings of advisors who had thwarted her. When the Pope's annulment of his first marriage didn't come, Henry tried to appease Anne by making her Marquise of Pembroke, a title that came with a handsome income. But, no, Anne wanted it all—at the cost of hundreds of lives. Six centuries later, we're still asking: who *exactly* did she think she was?

Okay, on the one hand, you can admire Anne's pluck. Refusing a king had to have been dangerous business back in the Renaissance. Not many would have the nerve today (let alone the opportunity). Her seduction of Henry was solid Siren stuff. Still, there's such a thing as going too far. Had she been in love with Henry, there might have been *some* sense in it. Yet she couldn't even bother to be respectful. Anne got drunk with the power of her own attractions and lost control. Her Kittenish tantrums and pouts—deliciously challenging in the girl Henry hoped to woo—became intolerable in a wife who was failing to do her job. Let Anne be a warning to the Siren who's prone to conceit.

As a Siren, you already command the attention of every red-blooded man in the room. Must you have them all to yourself, just because you have the power to do so? The King has showered you with jewels and turned over the house in Tuscany—must history be made to satisfy your whim? Don't lose perspective. Revenge is a poor substitute for love. Know when what you're asking is sheer arrogance and greed. As they say, pride goeth before the fall. And a wise Siren always keeps her friends at court.

don't lose your head

Mary Stuart, Queen of Scots

1542–1587

Sex Kitten Siren

From the moment Mary Stuart took the Scottish throne, finding her a suitable husband became a national emergency. The country needed an heir, of course, but the real danger was posed by the beauteous Mary herself. She had "some enchantment, whereby men are bewitched"—provoking amorous overtures. A lord was beheaded for threatening her chastity. A soldier's lewd scribblings were intercepted at court. A poet repeatedly hid in her bedroom in the hope of declaring his love (executed too). Not to mention, the randy Queen was constantly on the brink of compromising herself. Suitable matches were proposed, but Mary's untamed heart made the call. Henry Stewart, Lord Darnley—her first cousin—was "the lustiest and best proportioned long man" she had ever seen. What better reason to marry him?

"All her misfortunes may be traced to her mistaking flashy attractions for solid worth," wrote a historian. In sexual thrall, Mary was incapable of seeing the truth. To all at court, it was abundantly clear: Darnley was angling to be King and operating at a moral deficit. He was little more than a handsome brute—far from a wise and appropriate consort. But for Mary, royal life was an extended fairytale in which Darnley was prince. Her advisors trembled when she happily turned over "her whole will to him." Yet, time and again, Mary proved that she never learned anything about men through experience. She was doomed to lead with her heart, and it eventually cost her her head.

Mary Stuart was the daughter of James V of Scotland and a French royal, Mary of Guise. Promised as a child to the future King Francis I, Mary grew up at French court. Sadly, her young husband died after only a year on the throne. Mary returned

don't be a pushover

Lucrezia Borgia

1480–1519

Companion Siren

"What failed at lunch will be successful at supper," whispered Cesare Borgia in his brother-in-law's ear. The wounded Duke lay helpless, recovering from an attack carried out by Cesare's thugs on the steps of St. Peter's Cathedral in Rome. To protect him, his wife Lucrezia hovered nearby—but to no avail. By that night, Duke Alphonso was dead, strangled in his bed while Lucrezia was out of the room. What would become of the young widow, who wrung her hands so piteously with grief? Within weeks, her spirits appeared to be fully restored. Months later, Lucrezia was betrothed—a match that would strengthen the Borgias chokehold on the duchies and fiefdoms of Italy.

Schemer . . . murderess . . . the greatest whore in all Rome? Or were the rumors pulsing through the city untrue? Was Lucrezia Borgia closer to a vacuous blonde? You think there's too much corruption today. Meet the Borgias of Renaissance Italy. Lucrezia was either an evil manipulator, or (my vote) a dizzy dame who was pushed around—the pawn of a family that would stop at nothing to control Italy. The question is: why did Lucrezia go along so willingly?

Lucrezia was the daughter of Rodrigo Borgia, a Catholic cardinal, and his mistress—also the parents of three Mafioso-like boys. Lucrezia "melted Rodrigo's heart" from the first. She was the curly-haired darling who could do no wrong. As she grew, her bearing was so elegant that "she hardly seemed to move" when she walked. Such a daughter could serve as political glue. Upon being named Pope Alexander VI (no kidding), Rodrigo married off Lucrezia at thirteen to Giovanni Sforza, Lord of Pesaro, to get Milan on his side.

cautionary tales **255**

Back then, a man in favor one day might be out the next. It wasn't so different from politics today. No longer of use to the Borgias, Sforza was asked by the Pope to step aside—or find himself face down in the Tiber River by nightfall. Lucrezia flipped. She'd become attached to Giovanni, but she didn't like it when her father and brothers disapproved. She was declared *virgo intacto* (a virgin), making Sforza *de facto* impotent. In his parting shot, Sforza let slip that the Pope "wished to keep Lucrezia for himself." His suggestion of incest escaped no one.

NEED TO KNOW DEPT.

Lucrezia's "ethereal blond looks" so captivated the poet Lord Byron in 1816 that he stole a strand of her hair out of a cabinet at the Ambrosian Library in Milan. Byron called Lucrezia's sixteen-year correspondence with poet Pietro Bembo "the prettiest love letters in the world." Lucrezia's reputation for evil was the inspiration for a play by Victor Hugo and an opera by Donizetti.

Lucrezia "quite liked her husbands, when she could keep them." Yet, she moved on to the next so cheerfully. Why? The popular view was that "she had a terrible compulsion to please" the Borgia men. She got herself off to a nunnery for a sulk, only to rush "to the feet of [His] Beatitude" when he called. "My husbands have been unlucky" was the most she ever mustered in the way of protest. Rather than stand up for herself, Lucrezia bent every which way to their will. What did she get for it? The sad epitaph, "daughter, bride and daughter-in-law of Alexander," and one of the foulest reputations in history.

Lucrezia's third and last husband, the Duke of Ferrara, was surprised to find his new wife so "docile and pliant," given her poisonous reputation in Rome. He was not half as loveable as the earlier Duke had been. Lucrezia shopped and became a patron of the arts. She had two passionate flirtations, one with the poet Pietro Bembo and the other with her dashing brother-in-law. Pious at the end, she took to wearing a hair shirt and died from complications of childbirth.

Lucrezia's Lesson

After Duke Alphonso's murder, Lucrezia wept 24/7. Her sorrow baffled the old Pope, who was incapable of understanding how a girl of twenty could be so upset. As was her wont, Lucrezia retreated to the nunnery, which irritated her father even more. As soon as an ambassador reported that the Pope "did not love her so much," Lucrezia caved to the emotional blackmail. In the time it takes to buy a new trousseau, she was with the program. It was off to Ferrara with her retinue.

Wasn't this the Renaissance, when men were men, and women were wallpaper? In fact, the Renaissance produced many warrior-like women, particularly from the circles the Borgias moved in. Lucrezia was one of the few women in Rome who might have defied the Pope successfully. But she bowed before the males of the house with ever-increasing readiness. She is ultimately a cautionary tale of what can happen when a Companion Siren loses her way, when pleasing men becomes more important than anything. Net, net, there's no swifter way for a Siren to lose power. She'll end up being treated like property.

The pushover is always finding excuses for men, even when they compromise *her* position. He lies, cheats, steals, and gets away with murder. She says he was driven to it by forces beyond his control. In her opinion, he's a man who's simply misunderstood by everyone. As they said of Lucrezia, it was part of "her destiny to be deluded." She could "never rise to judgment" of the men in her world.

Does your life begin when a man calls? Is his idea of Saturday night together actually a beer with the boys? Are the presents he gives you actually meant for himself, and are you pathetically grateful he remembered at all? The diagnosis is in. You've lost control of the remote. You are decidedly a pushover.

Know that the pushover doesn't do anyone any favors by staying eternally mum. Take back your power. Speak up. The Siren who inspires a little fear never hurt anyone. A man out of line is always begging to be reined in. Today, the excuses for putting up with a cad are far less persuasive than they were six centuries ago. If he's brutish and cruel, don't stick around, let alone defend him.

in closing

Never mind how perspectives on love have shifted through the centuries. What makes a Siren irresistible is primal. Yet the nuances of her powers are infinite. All Sirens, of course, have absolute faith in their power to attract. They worship the ground men walk on. Their vitality is boundless, but this is where their paths diverge. Each Siren has her own seductive DNA, and so will you.

Who started the rumor that men prefer their women blonde and dumb? Or dark, silent, and mysterious? The Siren repeatedly kicks sand in the face of these myths. What the great seductresses show us is that men deserve far more credit than they are given. Look around. Men like women who are smart, red-headed, volatile, and full of opinions. Or plump, funny, blonde, and independent. Sometimes they like them boyish and fearless—or wildly talented. Above all, men love the women who let them. It's the defensive dame who consistently loses out.

One Siren may woo with her domestic charms, while another slays them with her sure instincts on the floor of the stock exchange or out on the hunting field. The Goddess Siren plays hard to get, while her sister, the Companion, wins by eagerly jumping into love the moment he asks her to. Between Beryl Markham and Jennie Jerome is a chasm of difference. Pamela Harriman and Cleopatra don't share seductive methodologies, let alone millennia. My grandmother and my mother—both world-class seductresses—approached men and love in their very own persuasive ways. It's a wide open field for the Siren who's creative.

As I've gotten to know these remarkable women, I've been consistently awed by their bravery. They are Sirens who have stood by their men, or had the courage to walk away when they had to. Some never married—Ninon de Lenclos, Queen Elizabeth I, and Coco Chanel, for instance. But not one ever lost her colossal confidence or let societal expectations dictate who she was. All adamantly refused to be pigeonholed. "I know I have the body of a weak and feeble woman," said Elizabeth I, as she led her troops into war, "but I have the heart and stomach of a king."

Eva Perón encouraged me to buy my first full-length mink. Zelda Fitzgerald showed me how a Siren can marshal her power by playing the field. After spending time with Pamela Harriman, I learned how to initiate the intimate conversation in a crowd—what came to be known as being "Pamelized." Carole Lombard proved that being funny is sexier than the barest skin. Through Mae West's example, I rethought pillow talk, and Nigella Lawson gave me the recipe to seduce.

It has been my singular honor to spend time among these Sirens while writing *Simply Irresistible*. I have often felt they were looking over my shoulder and cheering me on. Their words are as wise and alive as when they left their lips. Their spirits are now a part of me— forever. I hope they will become a part of you.

acknowledgments

When you begin writing a book, particularly if it's your first, you have no real idea of how wild the ride will be—or how important your family and friends, and even the families of your friends, will be when you are stumped for ideas or harboring the suspicion that you've gotten hopelessly lost. For their patient reading, advice, observations, cheer, advocacy, support, and/or listening skills, I'd like to thank Emily Beck, Bob Doerr, Nancy Fee, Lane Gifford, Lee Gifford, Enid and Steve Gifford, Grace Harvey and Jack Tigue, Whit Johnston, Anne Kay, Marla Musick, Wendy Osher, Hope Rogers, Liz Smith, Pam Taylor, Alexandra Weems, and Sally Wiggin, as well as my brothers, Lawrence White and Steve White, their wives Beth White and Alice Cooke, and my late father, Bonsal White. I'd particularly like to thank Adrian Zackheim for being an early believer who stepped up to the plate and for opening many, many doors that would otherwise have been closed to me. I am grateful to Barbara Bergeron and Tina Hoerenz for their keen editorial eyes. I thank Christy Fletcher and Bridie Clark for their help in developing the book's structure, and Brian deLorey and Peter Gay for suggesting many of the extraordinary women readers will find here. All of which leads me to my talented editor, Diana von Glahn, who instantly responded to the idea for *Simply Irresistible*, championed it, and understood exactly how I envisioned it. My sincere thanks to Amy Williams, my agent, for her tireless representation; to Susan Van Horn for her rich and humorous book design; and to Susan Oyama for her spot-on picture research. My thanks also go to Craig Herman and Seta Bedrossian Zink for their much-needed advice and promotional work. And, of course, I'd be nothing without those Sirens, past and present, whose lives have inspired me—from Cleopatra and Jennie Jerome to my mother and grandmother, Mollie Brent Johnston Lucas and Mathilde Manly Kernan, as well as Amanda Switzer, Esther Schweitzer, and Georgie Manly. Finally, all importantly, I want to thank Paul Dixon, whose unstinting encouragement and belief in dreams helped me achieve my own.

books and databases consulted for
Simply Irresistible

The Age of Conversation by Benedetta Craveri (New York Review of Books, 2005)

Alma Mahler or the Art of Being Loved by Françoise Giroud (Oxford University Press, 1991)

Angelina Jolie: Angel in Disguise by Edgar McKay (Icon Press, 2005)

Anne Boleyn by Norah Lofts (Coward, McCann & Geoghegan, Inc., 1979)

Becoming Mae West by Emily Wortis Leider (Da Capo Press, 1997)

Biography Resource Center, Gale Databases

The Bombshell Manual of Style by Loren Stover (Hyperion, 2001)

The Book of Courtesans: A Catalogue of Their Virtues by Susan Griffin (Broadway Books, 2001)

Carole Lombard: The Hoosier Tornado by West D. Gehring (Indiana Historical Society Press, 2003)

Catherine the Great by Henri Troyat, translated by Joan Pinkham (Penguin Books, 1977)

Chanel: A Woman of Her Own by Axel Madsen (Henry Holt and Company, 1990)

Cleopatra by Michael Grant (Castle Books, 2004)

Cleopatra and Rome by Diana E. E. Kleiner (The Belknap Press of Harvard University Press, 2005)

The Complete Claudine by Colette (Farrar, Straus & Giroux, 1956)

Courtesans by Katie Hickman (William Morrow, 2003)

Dangerous Muse: The Life of Lady Caroline Blackwood by Nancy Schoenberger (Da Capo Press, 2001)

The Divine Sarah: The Life of Sarah Bernhardt (Alfred A. Knopf, 1991)

The Duchess of Windsor: The Uncommon Life of Wallis Simpson by Greg King (Citadel Press, 1999)

Elizabeth and Mary: Cousins, Rivals, & Queens by Jane Dunn (Alfred A. Knopf, 2004)

Emma Hamilton by Nora Lofts (Coward, McCann & Geoghegan, Inc., 1978)

Evita: First Lady by John Barnes (Grove Press, 1978)

Evita: The Real Life of Eva Perón by Nicholas Fraser and Marysa Navarro (W. W. Norton, 1996)

Feast by Nigella Lawson (Hyperion, 2004)

Garbo by Barry Paris (Alfred A. Knopf, 1994)

Gone with the Wind by Margaret Mitchell (The Macmillian Company, 1936)

Great Dames: What I Learned from Older Women by Marie Brenner (Three Rivers Press, 2000)

His Secret Self by Bob Berkowitz (Simon & Schuster, 1997)

The Honest Courtesan: Veronica Franco, Citizen and Writer in Sixteenth-Century Venice by Margaret F. Rosenthal (The University of Chicago Press, 1992)

How to Talk with Practically Anybody About Practically Anything by Barbara Walters (Doubleday & Company, Inc., 1970)

Jacqueline Bouvier Kennedy Onassis: A Life by Donald Spoto (St. Martin's Press, 2000)

Jennie: The Life of Lady Randolph Churchill by Ralph G. Martin (two volumes) (New American Library, 1969)

   The Romantic Years (1854-1895)

   The Dramatic Years (1895-1921)

Lady Randolph Churchill by Anita Leslie (Lancer Books, 1969)

Life of the Party: The Biography of Pamela Digby Churchill Hayward Harriman by Christopher Ogden (Little, Brown, and Company, 1994)

The Lives of Beryl Markham by Errol Trzebinski (W. W. Norton & Company, 1993)

Lola Montez: A Life by Bruce Seymour (Yale University Press, 1996)

Lucrezia Borgia by Maria Bellonci (Orion Books Ltd., 2003)

Mademoiselle Libertine: A Portrait of Ninon de Lanclos by Edgar H. Cohen (Houghton Mifflin, 1970)

Marilyn Monroe: The Biography by Donald Spoto (HarperPaperbacks, 1993)

Mata Hari: A True Story by Russell Warren Howe (Dodd, Mead & Company, 1986)

Nicole Kidman: The Biography by Lucy Ellis & Bryony Sutherland (Aurum Press Ltd., 2002)

Nigella Lawson by Gilly Smith (Barricade Books, 2006)

Piaf by Simone Berteaut (Dell Publishing, Inc., 1979)

The Power of Style by Annette Tapert & Diana Edkins (Crown Publishers Inc., 1994)

ProQuest Research Library

Rage for Fame: The Ascent of Clare Boothe Luce by Sylvia Jukes Morris (Random House, 1997)

Reflected Glory: The Life of Pamela Churchill Harriman by Sally Bedell Smith (Simon & Schuster, 1996)

Secrets of the Flesh: A Life of Colette by Judith Thurman (Ballantine Books, 1999)

Seductress: Women Who Ravished the World and Their Lost Art of Love by Betsy Prioleau (Viking, 2003)

Slim: Memories of a Rich and Imperfect Life by Slim Keith with Annette Tapert (Simon & Schuster, 1990)

Sophia Loren: A Biography by Warren G. Harris (Simon & Schuster, 1998)

Susan Sarandon by Marc Shapiro (Prometheus Books, 2001)

Susan Sarandon: A True Maverick by Betty Jo Tucker (Hats Off Books, 2004)

Tallulah! The Life & Times of a Leading Lady by Joel Lobenthal (Reganbooks, 2004)

Tina Turner: Breaking Every Rule by Mark Bego (Taylor Trade Publishing, 2003)

The Uncrowned Queen: Life of Lola Montez by Ishbel Ross (Harper & Row, 1972)

Vatsyayana Kamasutra, translated by Wendy Doniger & Sudhir Kakar (Oxford University Press, 2002)

The Wilder Shores of Love by Lesley Blanch (Carroll & Graf Publishers, Inc., 1954)

The Windsor Knot: Charles, Camilla and the Legacy of Diana by Christopher Wilson (Pinnacle Books, 2002)

A Woman Named Jackie by C. David Heyman (Carol Communications, 1989)

Zelda: The Real Love Story of the Century by Nancy Milford (Avon Books, 1970)

index

art credits

Cover: *Leila*, detail, 1892, Sir Frank Dicksee (1853-1928), Private Collection. © The Fine Art Society, London, UK/The Bridgeman Art Library.

AP IMAGES: pp. 21, 27, 114, 180, 208, 239

Art Resource, NY:
p. 53: *Cyclists*, 1891. National Archives, London. © HIP
p. 254: *Lucrezia Borgia*, detail,1860-61, Dante Gabriel Rossetti. © Tate Gallery, London

The Bridgeman Art Library:
p. 12: *Ulysses and the Sirens*, detail, 1910, by Herbert James Draper. © Leeds Museums and Galleries (City Art Gallery), UK.
p. 23: *The Birth of Venus*, detail, c.1485, tempera on canvas, by Sandro Botticelli. Galleria degli Uffizi, Florence, Italy, Giraudon.
p. 33: *Lovers in a Café*, panel, Gotthardt Johann Kuehl (1850-1915). Berko Fine Paintings, Knokke-Zoute, Belgium.
p. 43: *Lilith*, detail, 1887, John Collier. © Atkinson Art Gallery, Southport, Lancashire, UK.
p. 63: *Diana Returning from the Hunt*, detail, c.1616, Peter Paul Rubens. Gemaeldegalerie Alte Meister, Dresden, Germany. © Staatliche Kunstsammlungen Dresden.
p. 77: *A Sea Spell*, detail, 1875-77, Dante Gabriel Rossetti. Fogg Art Museum, Harvard University Art Museums, USA, Gift of Grenville L. Winthrop, Class of 1886.
p. 91: *Anthony and Cleopatra*, 1883, by Sir Lawrence Alma-Tadema. © Private Collection.
p. 99: Caricature of Lola Montes dancing in front of King Ludwig I of Bavaria, lithograph, c.1847, German School. Musee de la Ville de Paris, Musee Carnavalet, Paris, France, Archives Charmet.
p. 109: *The Reception* or, *L'Ambitieuse* (Political Woman), c.1883-85, James Jacques Joseph Tissot. Albright Knox Art Gallery, Buffalo, New York, USA.
p. 121: Sarah Bernhardt in costume, c.1860, photograph by Nadar. Bibliotheque de L'Arsenal, Paris, France, Giraudon.
p. 133: *La Belle Dame Sans Merci*, detail, exh.1902, Sir Frank Dicksee (1853-1928). © Bristol City Museum and Art Gallery, UK.
p. 167: *Leila*, detail, 1892, Sir Frank Dicksee (1853-1928), Private Collection. © The Fine Art Society, London, UK.
p. 179: *Portrait of Catherine II*, detail, c.1770, Fedor Stepanovich Rokotov. Hermitage, St. Petersburg, Russia.
p. 198: *Pleading*, detail, 1876, Sir Lawrence Alma-Tadema. © Guildhall Art Gallery, City of London.
p. 225: *The Siren*, detail, 1900, John William Waterhouse. Private Collection.
p. 244: *Disappointed Love*, detail, 1821, Francis Danby. Victoria & Albert Museum, London, UK.
p. 247: *Anne Boleyn*, detail, French School, (16th century). Musee Conde, Chantilly, France, Lauros /Giraudon.
p. 250: M25 *Mary, Queen of Scots*, enamel on ivory by William Bone, Senior. © Wallace Collection, London, UK.